Going to College

Going to College

How Social, Economic, and Educational Factors Influence the Decisions Students Make

Don Hossler,
Jack Schmit,
and Nick Vesper

The Johns Hopkins University Press
Baltimore & London

Printed in the United States of America on acid-free paper
9 8 7 6 5 4 3 2 1

The Johns Hopkins University Press
2715 North Charles Street
Baltimore, Maryland 21218-4363
www.press.jhu.edu

Library of Congress Cataloging-in-Publication Data will be found at the end of this book.
A catalog record for this book is available from the British Library.

ISBN 0-8018-6000-8
ISBN 0-8018-6001-6 (pbk.)

In loving memory of Shirley
D. H.

To Sharon, my wife and friend,
and to our daughters, Natasha, Nicole, Amber, and Abigail
J. S.

To Jeannine
N. V.

Contents

Figures

Acknowledgments

Our longitudinal study and this resulting book would not have been possible without the long-term support of the Lilly Endowment and the Indiana Career and Postsecondary Advancement Center (ICPAC). We owe a deep debt of gratitude to Lilly Endowment vice president for education, Ralph Lundgren, and to Gail Dorman, our grant officer. On countless occasions the staff at ICPAC provided technical support, staff time, and (during the first two critical years) financial support for this research. We offer a special thank you to Scott Gillie, director of ICPAC, to Leo Fay, Professor Emeritus in the School of Education, to Roger Farr, Chancellors' Professor and director of the Center for Reading and Language Studies, and to Debbie Englert and Karla Farnsley.

We also thank Clyde Ingle, former comissioner for higher education in Indiana, and Karen Rasmussen, associate commissioner for planning and policy studies. ICPAC is the creation of the Commission for Higher Education. Clyde and Karen recognized early the potential benefits to policy makers of better understanding how the youth of Indiana develop post–high school plans.

Gary Bouse, who was for several years a project coordinator, was integral to the success of our study. During that time he conducted interviews, maintained financial records, and organized most of the project's key logistical elements. Frances Stage, professor of educational leadership and policy studies and associate dean of the School of Education at Indiana University, was also involved in several early reports resulting from this study.

In addition to Gary Bouse, other graduate students enrolled in the higher education program at Indiana University assisted with interviews, survey design, and analysis of data. They include Caitlan Anderson, Mark Bateman, Patti Boyd, Scott Brown, Hassan Chaharalang, Collete Chickeras, Cathy Clark, Randy Dodge, Patty Harned, John Hayek, Peggy Jennings, Jin Kang, Jack

Matkin, Jerry Olson, Andrea Paulus, Linda Pearson, Paul Schimmele, Jeff Weber, and Sara Westfall.

To protect the anonymity of the high schools and of the students and parents who participated in our study, we cannot name them or the guidance counselors who provided countless hours of assistance. Nevertheless, we are grateful to them for making this study possible.

Going to College

Going to College

Introduction

> *I can't remember when I* didn't *plan to go to college. Some of my earliest memories as a child are of my mother telling me that I would go to college when I got older.*
>
> High school sophomore

> *I wanted to look at schools in Ohio, but my mother told me that there were plenty of good public universities right here in Indiana.*
>
> High school junior

> *Of course I want Michael to go to college, but I don't know where he got the idea that we'll be able to take care of all his expenses.*
>
> Mother of a high school sophomore

> *How am I ever supposed to make up my mind? I keep getting all of this admissions stuff, and I have no idea which college would be best for me!*
>
> High school senior

> *In my senior year I decided I really did want to try to go to a college, but I had not taken enough of the right courses in high school. And there was no way I could get admitted anywhere.*
>
> High school senior

American families widely believe that nearly everyone in a modern society should obtain some form of postsecondary education. But many high school graduates do not in fact continue their education after high school. Other students plan to attend college through most of their high school years but then, for a variety of reasons, delay matriculation or never enroll.[1] Among students who do attend college, some cannot recall a time when they did not plan to go to college, while others decide as late as a week before the beginning of the academic year to attend. Still other students decide to attend college and discover too late that they did not take the appropriate courses.

For students who have always planned to continue their formal education beyond high school, their most difficult decisions are which college to attend and how to finance their education. No single path through these decisions exists. For some students, decisions about college seem simple, linear, and predictable; for others, the process is idiosyncratic and unpredictable.

In this book, we explore how students and their parents negotiate these important decisions. We examine how students confront decisions regarding continuing their education after high school and the career paths they pursue. During their high school years they begin to make important transitions into adulthood and find themselves making important decisions, although decision making is an activity in which they have had little practice or experience.

The decision about going to college is one of the first major noncompulsory decisions made by American adolescents and is an important marker in their transition from the final stages of childhood to the first steps of adulthood. These decisions have a lasting impact on the careers, livelihoods, and lifestyles of individual Americans and of society as a whole. The collective effects of individual decisions influence the health and vitality of the economy and society. In addition, these decisions enormously affect the postsecondary system of education. Yet for all of the importance of the outcome of the college decision-making process that students and their families go through, this process has received surprisingly little attention.

In this book, we rectify this situation. We report on a nine-year longitudinal study of the postsecondary educational decision-making process among a sample of high school students in Indiana. Using data collected from surveys of large numbers of Indiana students as well as from interviews with a small number of students and parents, we examine the influences on, the characteristics of, and the outcomes of their decisions. We consider the role that parents, peers, teachers, counselors, and college marketing activities play in this process. And we analyze the educational aspirations of students and their subsequent educational achievements. Although we also examine the factors and experiences that influence the decisions of students who do not attend college, our primary focus is on those who go on to some form of formal postsecondary education.

---

1. For simplicity, we use the term *college* throughout this book to mean any type of postsecondary educational institution.

This book is organized into four parts, each comprising two chapters. The opening chapters of the first three parts relate the experiences of eight students who tell how they made their post–high school decisions. Among these eight students are individuals who were always sure they were going to college and individuals whose plans shifted throughout their high school years. Some students' plans continued to shift even after they graduated from high school. Students who did not continue their education after high school and a student who dropped out of our study and out of high school are included among the eight.

The second chapter in each of the first three parts is a companion piece, reporting findings and conclusions from surveys and interviews employed during our longitudinal study. The eight students' stories make the decision-making process come alive, and the reporting of empirical analyses provides the evidence necessary to arrive at useful conclusions and recommendations.

The two chapters of part 4 explore what happened to some of the students in our study after they graduated from high school. We interviewed a subsample of fifty-six students after they had been out of high school for approximately seven months and again about four years after they had graduated from high school. We compare the aspirations of these students with what actually happened to them to enhance our understanding of the college decision-making process.

The final chapter reports our conclusions and recommendations and the appendix provides an overview of the relevant theories and previous research that informed this study.

THE COLLEGE DECISION-MAKING PROCESS

Students, Parents, and Guidance Counselors

The decisions that students make about college have a lasting impact on their lives. Increased education leads to higher salaries, longer working lives, more career mobility, and a higher quality of life (Bowen, 1977; Leslie and Brinkman, 1988; Pascarella and Terenzini, 1991). Ingrained in American society is a belief that higher education is an investment in human capital (DeYoung, 1989), which benefits the individuals who earn college degrees. Leslie and Brinkman (1988), in their metanalysis of individual rates of return on higher education, conclude that college graduates earn 12–15 percent more than the average high school graduate when high school and college graduates of similar ability are compared. College graduates are less likely to be unemployed for long periods, and they are less likely to miss work for prolonged periods because of health problems. College graduates also report being happier and more satisfied with life (Bowen, 1977).

Given the importance of the college decision, it is surprising that students and parents are not offered more assistance in making it. Although a profusion of college guidebooks and rating guides have been published in recent years, these books are not designed to help students and their families move through the various stages of the decision-making process (see Hossler and Litten, 1993). Indeed, these guides would be much more helpful if the information in them were organized in ways that more closely parallel how high school students structure their college decision-making process.

Understanding the college decision-making process can also be useful to high school guidance counselors, whose role is to provide assistance to students and families. In many schools, students enrolled in the eighth or ninth grade begin a formal (though very limited) curriculum of career and educational planning while enrolled in a civics or sociology course. Yet most guidance counselors have had little exposure to college planning. Boyer (1987) was highly critical of the negligible impact of high school guidance counselors in preparing high school students to make the transition from secondary to postsecondary education. In a large study of high school students in Indiana, Orfield and Paul (1993) concluded that students needed more information about college options and better high school guidance services. A better understanding of the college decision-making process might help high school guidance counselors guide students and families more effectively.

Public Policy Makers

Research on college decision making can lead to new public policy initiatives that might enable federal and state governments to provide college education in a more cost-effective manner and, simultaneously, to increase the nation's stock of educated workers. Public policy makers have long supported education as a vehicle for economic development and as a necessity for a strong democracy. These assumptions explain the interest among public policy makers in increasing the educational achievements of citizens.

Although economists debate the nature and extent of the economic benefits of higher education for society and individuals, most of them agree that individual states, and indeed the nation, benefit from a better educated citizenry (McGregor, 1994). These benefits include workforce planning and enhanced economic competitiveness, government revenues, and social and economic equality. Not only do individuals who earn college degrees earn more money and have more career mobility, but also private businesses and industries hire more college graduates and sell more goods to them. In addition, all levels of government can collect more taxes from individuals with more education. During the 1950s and 1960s, economists concluded that increased levels of education among American workers had made substantial contributions to increased productivity and growth in business and industry (Schultz, 1961; Becker, 1964). Denison (1971) estimated that, between 1929 and 1957, 23 percent of the growth in national income could be allocated to improvements in education.

One of the consequences of economic growth and productivity has been the increase in taxes paid by business and industry. Public policy makers have also used financial incentives such as the GI Bill to increase college enrollments and to influence the size and composition of the labor market. Federal financial aid policies, such as the National Defense Student Loan, have also tried to influence choices of student majors to meet the anticipated needs of the labor market.

Many advocates of a college education argue that the benefits to society go beyond the monetary. After reviewing the research on societal benefits stemming from increased levels of education, Bowen (1977) and more recently Pascarella and Terenzini (1991) concluded that college graduates are better citizens: they are more likely to vote, more likely to assume civic leadership positions, more likely to utilize new technologies, more likely to support advanced education for their children and their communities, and less likely to be involved in criminal activities.

A college education is also considered a social escalator for many disadvantaged groups in American society. Many social critics and public policy makers support increased levels of education for all citizens to redress past social injustices and to improve social equity. Disadvantaged groups include the economically deprived, low-socioeconomic-status families, ethnic minorities, and women. Public policy makers have supported programs to increase the numbers of low-income individuals, women, ethnic minorities, and other underrepresented groups enrolling in college.

These seemingly compelling reasons for supporting college education, however, have not gone unchallenged. The rate of return to individuals is also influenced by nonegalitarian factors such as students' family background, their choice of major, the status of the college they attend, their ethnicity, and their gender (Jencks et al., 1972; Leslie and Brinkman, 1988; Pascarella and Terenzini, 1991). Recently, critics of unbridled faith in the human capital model have also challenged the assertion that increased levels of education provide economic benefits to the nation; Walberg (1990) found an inverse relationship between levels of education and economic productivity in several industrialized countries. Few scholars doubt, however, that higher levels of education are related to increased economic prosperity at the local and regional levels (Leslie and Brinkman, 1988).

Although Jencks et al. (1972) concluded that education does improve social equality, Anderson and Hearn (1992), in a more detailed analysis, suggested that not all Americans benefit equally from increased education. They demonstrate that while the outcomes of higher education have improved for women and ethnic minorities, returns continue to lag severely for those from lower classes.

Despite these doubts about the relationship between education and economic well-being, most public policy makers continue to support increased public access to postsecondary education. They may do so because they believe in the individual and social benefits, or they may do so simply because the political costs of not supporting increased access are too great. Because of their differing roles in postsecondary education, federal and state policy makers have at times pursued different strategies to influence college enrollment decisions. To date, the principal federal public policy mechanism for intervening in the college enrollment decisions of traditional-age students has been through student financial aid, both grants and loans. By lowering the net cost of attendance to students and their families, federal policy makers have sought to enhance students' access to and choice of college. States have typically had three policy approaches: low-cost tuition, state financial aid and loan programs, and more recently legislation to encourage savings and prepaid tuition plans.

As competition for state treasury dollars grew and the federal deficit increased, federal and state policy makers found they could no longer afford generous financial aid programs or publicly subsidized low-cost tuition. However, public policy makers and the public are unwilling to allow postsecondary education to be affordable only to the middle and upper classes.

A better understanding of the college decision-making process will not resolve many of these issues, but it will provide insights that can lead to new public policy initiatives. For example, a better understanding of the role of parents and the impact of information on the decision-making process could help guide public policies to provide more incentives for college savings among middle-class families. An improved understanding of the decision-making process may enable local and state policy makers to devise more effective and more timely information programs about postsecondary education. These programs might encourage more low-income and first-generation students to continue their formal education beyond high school. Additionally, new insights into college decision making might enable states to devise incentives to reduce the out-migration of talented students to other states, increasing a state's pool of highly trained workers. These and other initiatives could play a role in resolving some of our public policy dilemmas.

College Policy Makers

For college policy makers, interest in the college decision-making process is the outcome of enlightened self-interest. Student enrollments are the lifeblood of colleges. We have found that class size and the individual attributes of enrolled students at colleges define many important characteristics of individual campuses (Hossler and Bean, 1990). At both public and private institutions, total student enrollment typically accounts for 30–90 percent of all revenue. Furthermore, average class rank of entering students, average Scholastic Aptitude Test (SAT) scores, and number of in-state and out-of-state students are common indicators of institutional prestige.

The ability of women's colleges, men's colleges, and historically black colleges to enroll a sufficient number of women, men, and black students, respectively, is critical to their distinctive missions. Similarly, for church-related colleges to maintain their ties with sponsoring church groups, often it is crucial for them to enroll large numbers of students from sponsoring denominations. With the declining number of high school graduates during the past two decades and the upward spiral of college costs, few should be surprised that college policy makers have sought to better understand the reasons students chose to enroll in their schools.

Several colleges have been able to exercise more influence than others over their enrollments through well-crafted institutional research. For example, the College Board has developed surveys and data bases that can be used by individual colleges to better understand their market position. Boston College, under the leadership of Jack Maguire and later Robert Lay (see Maguire and Lay, 1981), and Carleton College, with the assistance of Larry Litten and colleagues (see Litten, Sullivan, and Brodigan, 1984), are examples of how college market research has been used to guide campus marketing strategies. Campus-based research studies continue to guide college marketing and recruitment practices. They have strengthened the ability of some colleges to attract and retain students and, in addition, have enhanced our understanding of the college decision-making process.

At some private colleges, the cost of student financial aid accounts for nearly 30 percent of the education and general category of their budgets. The use of both need-based and no-need financial aid has become a common and expensive form of price discounting for private colleges. As public colleges increasingly opt for high-tuition and high-aid strategies to cope with declines in state support, they too are investing more money in college financial aid. Schools have developed various strategies to meet this challenge. Rensselaer Polytechnical Institute, DePauw University, and the University of Dayton, for example, have used multivariate analytic techniques to target financial aid awards to segments of their applicant pool, thus increasing their yield of enrolled students. DePauw has dramatically increased the number of African American students through targeted financial aid awards.

Well-crafted studies of the effects of net cost and student financial aid upon college decision making can enable college policy makers to more effectively target their financial aid funds and to set tuition rates that will help colleges achieve their enrollment goals. By extending their understanding of college decision making, college and public policy makers will be able to target scarce financial resources more effectively.

THE LONGITUDINAL STUDY

The longitudinal study, which is the foundation of the research for this book, was conducted in the state of Indiana between 1986 and 1994.(For a description of the sample, research methods, surveys, interview protocols, and analytical methods employed, see the appendix.) Using a cluster sampling technique, 4,923 students and their parents were surveyed in January 1987. Between 1987 and 1990, these students and their parents, or smaller subsamples, were surveyed eight times. In addition, a subsample of 56 students and their parents were interviewed in depth nine times between 1989 and 1994. Insufficient funding in 1986–88 affected our design. No interviews were conducted in the students' freshman year (1986–87). During their sophomore year (1987–88), we conducted separate group interviews with students and parents. However, we had funding to send only one survey to students and parents that year. After carefully reviewing our findings, we found that the concerns and decisions of sophomores and juniors were sufficiently similar that results of our analyses for students in the tenth and eleventh grades could be combined.

All students were first-year students in high school when the study began and had been out of high school for four years when the study concluded. By 1994, when our last interview was conducted, some students were college seniors, others had been in and out of more than one college, others had permanently dropped out, while others were still planning to enroll for the first time. Some students were working, some had joined the military, some had married.

We advise readers to use caution in applying the findings from this study across states. The average parental income and educational levels for Indiana families rank in the bottom half of the fifty states. Unlike many states, Indiana does not have a large community college system, limiting students' college options. Furthermore, unlike states such as Massachusetts and Illinois, Indiana lacks nationally known and highly selective private colleges, like the University of Chicago, Harvard, and Amherst. This also limited students' options. Finally, our study did not include large numbers of high-ability students, a limitation that undoubtedly influenced our findings (see appendix).

A MODEL OF COLLEGE CHOICE

The development of educational aspirations and the achievement of those aspirations has long been of interest to sociologists. This line of study is referred to as research on status attainment. Traditionally, however, sociologists have not used models of status attainment to examine in detail the college decision-making process. Indeed, studies of status attainment have focused more on the development of educational aspirations than upon the achievement of those aspirations.

Recently, scholars have developed models of student college choice that consider how traditional-age students go about realizing their educational aspirations. We use one of these models—the Hossler and Gallagher (1987) three-stage model of college choice—to organize our findings. This model posits three stages in the college-choice process: predisposition, search, and choice.

Predisposition refers to the plans students develop for education or work after they graduate from high school. Students' family background, academic performance, peers, and other high school experiences influence the development of their post–high school educational plans.

The *search* stage includes students' discovering and evaluating possible colleges in which to enroll. The model posits that students' searches help them determine what characteristics they need and which colleges offer them (is the college residential or commuting? is it large or small? are the campus facilities adequate? does the faculty concentrate on teaching or on research?). Hossler, Braxton, and Coopersmith (1989) noted that little research has been done on the search stage of college decision making.

In the *choice* stage, students choose a school from among those they have considered. Some students consider only one school, perhaps one that is close to home so they can commute. As the academic performance of students and the socioeconomic status of their families increase, the number of colleges considered also increases. High-ability students might apply to five or more colleges throughout the states.

RESEARCH QUESTIONS

Six broad research questions were explored in our nine-year study, questions that emerged from both previous status-attainment and college-choice research and from our study.

1. How do students develop postsecondary educational aspirations? To what extent do family background characteristics and student abilities determine the educational aspirations and achievements of students? To what extent do peers, schools, and access to information influence the development of educational aspirations? Are there critical time periods when students are prone to make decisions and close off other alternatives?

2. How do students find out about colleges? How active are students in seeking out information about colleges? Are the types of college that students consider determined by family background and student ability? Are the types of college that students consider determined accidentally or through a rational and logical search? To what extent do the marketing activities of colleges influence the schools that students consider?

3. How do students choose a college? What role do college marketing activities play in these choices? When do students make their choice? To what extent do social status and social capital determine the colleges students choose?

4. How do tuition costs and financial aid influence the college decision-making process? Do perceived costs and the likelihood of receiving financial aid influence the colleges students choose? How much do students and their parents know about tuition costs and student financial aid? To what extent do students and parents believe that increased financial aid would influence their enrollment decisions?

5. Do students realize their postsecondary educational aspirations? To what do they attribute their educational and career paths after graduating from high school? Are they satisfied with their decisions?

6. What is the parents' role in students' college choices? Does the parents' role change as students move through the process? How can parents help students through the process?

PART ONE

The Predisposition toward Going to College

Chapter 1 introduces the eight students whom we followed for nine years, from the ninth grade until four years after their graduation from high school. We did not begin interviews for this study until these students were high school juniors, so to introduce these students as ninth graders we rely on two types of information. Primarily, we draw upon answers the students and their parents provided on surveys they completed in the ninth grade. Some surveys from later years included questions about earlier years, and in some cases we use these responses. In addition, we use information that students and parents provided in interviews as they reflected upon their first year of high school. The differences in the specific information included in the narratives about each student stem from missed interviews or incompleted questionnaires.

As you become acquainted with these eight students, key issues are evident that merit attention. The results from our research (Bateman, 1990; Hossler and Stage, 1992; Stage and Hossler, 1989) and previous studies on the formation of educational aspirations indicate that the role of parents is especially important (Galotti and Mark, 1994; Hossler, Braxton and Coopersmith, 1989; Paulsen, 1990; Sewell and Shah, 1978). We also introduce several parental involvement themes that emerged from our study and that provide a framework for more research on the parental role in students' college choice (Schmit and Hossler, 1995).

In addition to parents, student academic success plays a significant role in students' college choice, as does the influence of friends (peers) and the high school track in which the students are enrolled (Hearn, 1984; McDonough, 1997). Less attention has been given to when students begin to formulate their postsecondary plans and how they explore their options (Hossler, Braxton, and Coopersmith, 1989).

In chapter 2, we discuss our empirical findings on the predisposition stage of college choice. This includes the variables that influence the formation of plans to go to college, the degree of certainty students have about their plans at this early age, and how their plans evolve. We integrate our findings with previous work on these topics to provide a comprehensive overview of the predisposition stage of the college choice process.

1

Emerging College Aspirations

In this chapter, we introduce the ninth-grade high school students whose lives we followed for the ensuing nine years. We describe their school settings and their family backgrounds, discuss their initial career and educational plans, and highlight the interactions between these students and their parents. Although parents play a critical role in the predisposition stage of the college decision-making process, precisely how parental influence interacts with other student characteristics and experiences needs additional exploration.

Allison

In the ninth grade, Allison planned to get a job right after high school. She was an average student, earning mostly C's. Allison lived with her parents in a small town in northern Indiana, approximately sixty minutes from the cities of Gary and Hammond, part of the Chicago metropolitan area. Her mother was a high school graduate and worked as a clerk in a local convenience store; her father was also a high school graduate and worked on the loading dock of a trucking firm. Allison's parents reported a combined family income of between $35,000 and $39,999.

The high school that Allison attended enrolled a thousand students and is located in a residential area near the small downtown area of her town. The population of the town is heterogeneous, but all of the students at the high school are Euro-Americans. In the ninth grade, Allison was not very involved in high school activities.

Allison had an older sister, who was married and living nearby. The sister had not gone to college immediately after graduating from high school, but after working for the same trucking firm that their father worked for, she attended Ivy Tech State College and earned a two-year degree in computer science. She later worked at a shopping mall as an accountant and inventory specialist, taking part-time classes at nearby Valparaiso University. Allison's sister and parents encouraged Allison to go to college after high school, but in the ninth grade Allison had no educational aspirations beyond high school and was undecided about her career plans.

Even during Allison's ninth grade, Allison's mother was concerned about her daughter's lack of ambition and noted that Allison had few friends in school and that she usually came home after school and watched television. Allison reported that she did not talk to her parents or to her friends much about the future.

Allison's profile matches those of other students who did not continue their education after high school. Even though she had supportive parents and a sibling who took an interest in Allison's future, her average grades and lack of educational or career aspirations pointed to a probable decision to get a job immediately after high school.

Amy

In 1986–87, Amy was a C student in the ninth grade at a racially integrated high school in Indianapolis, the largest city in Indiana and also its state capital. Amy, an African American, was living with her mother; her parents were divorced, and we learned nothing about her father. Amy's mother was unemployed; from subsequent interviews with Amy, we learned that her mother had a history of mental instability, alcohol abuse, and drug abuse. Amy, the youngest child in her family, had two brothers and one sister. Her sister lived in Indianapolis; both brothers were in military service. An aunt, whom Amy was close to, was also in military service. In interviews, Amy told us that she sometimes lived with her mother and sometimes lived with her sister. Her family income could not be determined.

Amy's high school enrolled two thousand students when she was in ninth grade. She earned mostly B's and C's; she did not know whether she was enrolled in an academic or a vocational track. Although Amy indicated that she thought a great deal about her postsecondary school plans and talked to her friends about her future, in ninth grade, she was undecided about her plans after high school. She thought she would either get a job or enter military service.

Amy's profile fit that of other at-risk students. The lack of stability and parental support in Amy's life, along with her lack of goals and aspirations, were like those of other students in our sample who were unlikely to continue their education after high school. Our research team privately wondered if Amy would even manage to complete high school, given her difficult circumstances.

Jerome

Jerome, like Amy, lived in Indianapolis and attended an integrated high school (with an enrollment of 1,800). Jerome is African American. His father owned a small metalworking shop and his mother, who held a master's degree in social work, was a social worker in a high school. His father had graduated from high school but had not attended college. The family income was $50,000 to $60,000.

Jerome was the youngest of three children; his brother was three years older than him and his sister two years older. Jerome's mother, who was knowledgeable about postsecondary education and had strong opinions about Jerome's future and the kinds of college Jerome should be considering, attended all of the interviews we scheduled for parents during our longitudinal study. Jerome reported that his parents strongly encouraged him to attend college after high school.

In ninth grade, Jerome was an average student, earning primarily C's, and was enrolled in the academic track. Jerome reported that, during that year, he planned to attend a four-year college but that he felt as if many unrealistic expectations had been placed upon him because his older brother, Ray, who was a senior in high school at this time, was a school leader and had plans to go to college.

According to Jerome's mother, Jerome was good at math, and because of these skills she had been able to enroll him, in sixth grade, in a preengineering enrichment program offered by Purdue University. Although Jerome did not want to be an engineer and was uncertain about the career or major he wanted to pursue, the program did expose him to information about colleges, which he would draw on in subsequent years.

Overall, Jerome's college plans were not very well developed by the ninth grade. While Jerome's situation was not much different from many of his peers, we found his lack of future orientation surprising because of his mother's strong encouragement, his siblings' decisions about college, and his involvement in the Purdue program. The handful of other students in our study with similar attributes—at least one strongly encouraging parent who was a college graduate; older siblings who had graduated from, were enrolled in, or were preparing to enroll in college; and involvement in an enrichment program—were more focused than Jerome in the ninth grade.

Laura

In the ninth grade, Laura lived with her parents and her sister in a small town that was in transition to becoming a suburb of the larger city of Evansville. Laura's mother was a trained psychologist and worked part-time; her father was the city manager. They reported a combined income of $70,000 to $79,999. Laura's sister, who was three years older than Laura, was a strong student and was planning to enter either Valparaiso University or Butler University.

Laura's high school enrolled approximately 1,500 students, all of them Euro-Americans. In the ninth grade, Laura was active in her high school and community, belonging to church groups, school clubs, and the cheerleading team. She was a B student and planned to enroll in a four-year college immediately after high school. She received strong encouragement from her parents to continue her education after high school, but she talked more to her friends than to her parents about her post–high school plans. Laura thought about her plans after high school only moderately, which is typical for students in ninth grade. Her reason for going to college was to get a well-paying job. She planned to major in business or public affairs.

In the ninth grade, Laura already knew that she wanted to attend a residential college and not live at home, and her parents agreed. They also agreed that the academic reputation of the college would be the most important factor in her selection and that total costs and the availability of financial aid would be important considerations. Laura's parents had been saving for three to five years for the college educations of their daughters.

A college education was an important value in Laura's family, and unlike most of the parents in our study, Laura's parents had been saving for their children's college expenses, a tangible form of parental support and encouragement. As a result, Laura thought about the kind of college she might attend and even about how to finance her college education, a level of focus and specificity about college plans unusual for students in the ninth grade.

Sam

Sam was the only surviving child of a family living in Indianapolis. (Sam's older sister had been killed in an automobile accident five years earlier.) His parents were both high school graduates. His mother worked as a secretary in an insurance company; his father was a lathe operator in a tool manufacturing plant. Their combined income was approximately $35,000. Sam is a Euro-American and was enrolled in the same high school that Amy attended.

He was in the college preparation track and earned A's in all of his classes. Sam took the Scholastic Achievement Test (SAT) test as a ninth grader as part of a statewide effort at early identification of talented students. He never told us his score but acknowledged that he had done "very well."

Sam's parents strongly encouraged him to earn a four-year college degree after completing high school. They were, in fact, already saving for Sam's college expenses. Sam did plan to attend a four-year college immediately after high school, but he reported talking more to his friends about these plans than to his parents.

A small number of students in our sample were, like Sam, very focused on going on to college; many could not recall a time in their lives when they had not planned to go to college. Even in ninth grade, Sam wrote letters requesting information from colleges, having decided, along with some of his friends, to start learning more about colleges.

For Sam, the most important reason for going to college was to get a well-paying job and the most important criteria for selecting a college were its academic reputation and the length of time necessary to finish the degree program. He wanted to live at home or with relatives and attend a college in a metropolitan area within an hour from home.

The high level of parental support Sam enjoyed appeared to interact positively with his academic ability and early interest in college and a specific major. His early exploration of colleges made him much more knowledgeable about his college options than most of the students in our sample. Not going to college had never been an option for Sam. The only important question was where he would go. Unlike most of the students in our sample, Sam had an early start on answering this question.

Seth

Seth lived with his parents and younger sister in a small town outside of Fort Wayne. His father was a factory worker and his mother a cook in a restaurant. Seth's father and mother had both graduated from high school and reported an annual family income between $25,000 and $29,999. Seth was a B or C student in the ninth grade, very active in high school athletics, and moderately active in radio and television activities. The high school he attended had fewer than a thousand students and a totally Euro-American student body.

In the ninth grade, Seth did not think very much about his plans after high school, but he did think he might go to a vocational or technical school. His parents held similar aspirations for him. Seth talked mostly to his parents about his plans. His occupational interests included mechanical engineering, industrial production work, and the hospitality industry. Seth and his parents agreed that the most important reason for going to college was to get a well-paying job. Seth anticipated needing some financial aid to pay for college, even though his parents had been saving for his education for the past three to five years and were not sure he would need financial aid.

Both Seth and his parents indicated that they hoped he would attend a school within an hour from the family home. Seth's parents hoped he would live at home and go to school. Location and good teachers were the two most important criteria for choosing a school, according to Seth and his parents, with financial aid another consideration.

Seth's aspirations and thoughts about college mirrored those of many students in our sample who were either uncertain about their plans or who planned to attend a vocational school. These students typically did not think much about their future. Often, neither parents nor siblings had gone to college. The desire to stay close to home was also more common among students with lower educational aspirations.

Michelle

Michelle, an African American, attended high school in Fort Wayne, where she lived with her divorced mother. Her mother, who had attended high school but had not graduated, worked in a factory and earned between $10,000 and $14,999. Michelle had two older brothers, both in the military. Michelle did not often refer to her brothers throughout the nine-year period of our study, so we assumed they did not have a strong influence upon her college plans and subsequent decisions.

The high school Michelle attended had more than 2,500 students. During the time Michelle was in high school, Fort Wayne schools relied upon busing to achieve integration, and approximately 30 percent of the students enrolled in her school were African Americans. In the ninth grade, Michelle was a C student. She reported being involved in high school athletics, high school radio and television programs, and church activities. Michelle planned to enter a four-year college immediately after high school and to eventually earn a master's degree. During ninth grade, she thought a great deal about her plans after high school and talked, primarily to her friends, about her plans. After taking business classes, Michelle eventually became interested in a career in business. "In elementary I loved math. And it was like, the older I got, I found that it wasn't as easy as elementary style. But I kept at it. Then when I got into sixth grade, and they had little business classes and all that stuff. . . that's what I decided I want to do."

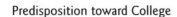

For Michelle and her mother, the most important reason to go to college was to get a well-paying job. For both, the most important characteristics in a college were a good academic reputation, good teachers, and being affiliated with a church. They agreed that Michelle should attend a residential college not more than two or three hours away from home, and both thought that financial aid would be necessary to pay for a college education.

In the ninth grade, Michelle was already thinking a good deal about her college plans and aspired to a master's degree. Her mother was very supportive of Michelle's plans. Michelle was already considering going to a private church-related college and thinking about needed financial assistance. Generally, in our research, we found these student and family characteristics were associated with students who subsequently achieved their goals. The only factors that were not consistent with a pattern of subsequent achievement were the educational level of Michelle's mother and the fact that Michelle was talking more to her peers than to her mother about her plans, factors that are explored in greater detail in chapter 3.

Todd

By the ninth grade, Todd had already determined that he did not want to continue his formal education after high school and planned, instead, to enter military service. Todd, a Euro-American, attended a large public high school in a small town in Indiana about two hours south of Indianapolis. Todd stood in contrast to other students in our study who did not plan to attend college, many of whom were uncertain of their plans.

Todd lived with his parents and an older brother, a senior in high school. Another brother had already graduated and had enlisted in the marines. Todd's mother worked as a retail clerk, his father in an automobile manufacturing plant. Both had graduated from high school and earned an income of $30,000 to $40,000. Unlike Seth, Todd talked primarily to his friends, not his parents, about his future plans. Although Todd's parents were supportive of him and of whatever he wanted to do, they did not seem to be a major influence on his plans.

Todd earned mostly C's in high school and had clearer goals in mind than other ninth-grade students in our sample. For the first three months after graduation, before he entered military service, he planned to hike the Appalachian Trail. Todd presents, therefore, a contrast to the stereotype of high school students who do not plan to attend a college as individuals without definite plans.

SUMMARY

Seven of the eight students—all except Amy—appeared to have had the support and encouragement of their parents. However, parental support alone was not enough to cause these ninth-grade students to develop firm plans for their futures. For some of these students (Amy, Sam, and Laura), conversations with friends also appeared to be important. Some were actively engaged in making plans for their futures. Others were at least formulating post–high school plans.

Sam, Laura, and Michelle had either thought about postsecondary plans or had engaged in activities related to them. Having clear personal goals or having siblings who had recently gone through the college choice process seemed to be important for these students. As might be expected, the absence of clear plans in the cases of Allison and Amy seems to have had the opposite effect.

In the following chapters, we trace these students' activities and decisions over the following nine years of their lives, exploring how family background, scholastic ability, parental encouragement, social context, information, and motivation influenced these students and the formation and pursuit of their educational and career aspirations. We examine the patterns that emerged and provide additional information for further research and policy development.

In the chapter 2, we summarize the statistical analyses of our sample and compare these findings with previous research to come to an understanding of the factors that affect student aspirations.

2

Influences on College Aspirations

The stories of the students in chapter 1 illustrate the rich variety in the college decision-making processes of high school students. But it is also possible to identify common themes among high school students in the predispostion stage. Statistical analyses and qualitative analytic procedures in our research provide insights into the variables that influence this stage.

In the first and second years of our research, we were interested in two questions. (1) Which individuals, background characteristics, or high school experiences have the greatest influence on the development of a predisposition among students to continue their education after high school? Parents, family structure, family income, parents' educational level, and students' achievement? What role do peers, teachers, and counselors play? Does student participation in high school activities have an effect on predisposition? And (2), are the educational plans of students well developed by the time students are first-year high school students? How much information do they have about college opportunities, about the costs of a college education, or about the financial aid system? What kinds of additional information do they need?

Using a series of surveys of and interviews with students and parents, we examined these questions in detail and present our findings in the order of their relative impact on the educational aspirations of students. In our analysis, we generally used multivariate statistical techniques, which enabled us to compare students of similar backgrounds and experiences; without large samples of students and the use of multivariate techniques, we would not have been able to untangle the effects of family income, parental encouragement, peers, and student achievement on students' predisposition for college. For example, Sam planned to attend a four-year college while Amy was undecided about her plans but leaned toward working or entering military service. Neither Sam's nor Amy's parents went to college. However, Sam's parents had a higher family income than Amy's mother, and Sam achieved better grades than Amy. Although multivariate statistical techniques did not explain the differences between Sam's and Amy's college plans, they did enable us to probe the effects of an array of variables.

With large numbers of students (there were nearly five thousand students in our sample), multivariate techniques permitted us to find students in the sample with similar characteristics, thus holding the relevant variables constant. When we found that some students planned to continue their education after high school and some did not, we searched for an explanation. If we find, for example, that students with similar levels of parental income and education were more likely to plan to go to college, we can conclude that this is an important variable. Multivariate statistical techniques permit these kinds of comparisons.

The ability of any type of analytical technique to explain sociological phenomena, however, should not be overstated. In this study—and indeed in any study of human behavior—our ability to provide a complete explanation of outcomes and actions is limited. In this study, we were able to isolate variables and experiences that influenced outcomes, but any explanation of the differences between Sam's and Amy's postsecondary plans will be incomplete at best.

For this longitudinal investigation, however, we were able to enrich the findings from the statistical analyses by including insights gained from our interviews with a subsample of fifty-six students and their parents. The data from these interviews were analyzed by looking for emergent themes, using procedures suggested by Miles and Huberman (1984) and Lincoln and Guba (1985). This approach permitted us to extend our understanding of the variables and experiences that predispose ninth graders to plan to go to college.

THE TIMING OF INTERVENTION

If parents, high school guidance counselors, and policy makers wish to influence the predisposition stage of college decision making, knowing when students solidify their decisions is helpful. Once students begin to articulate formal plans, it becomes more difficult to alter them.

Our research (Hossler and Stage, 1987) found that most high school students formalize their educational plans between eighth grade and tenth grade. Other studies (Parish, 1979; Stewart et al., 1987) concluded that the educational plans of students are not fully formed or at least are not completed until the tenth grade. By beginning our study when students were in the ninth grade, we were able to track the shifts in their plans over a period of time. Most of the students in our study made this decision when they were in eighth or ninth grade, which does not mean that the decision was irrevocable. As becomes evident in subsequent chapters, some students (like Laura) wavered throughout their high school years about their college plans. For others (like Sam), their plans did not change at all. Among the students in our study, 67 percent who decided in the eighth or ninth grade to go to college enrolled within a year after high school graduation. More than 80 percent of the ninth-grade students in our sample, along with their parents, reported that the most important reason for going to college was to be able to get a good job. This suggests that most ninth-grade students have primarily utilitarian reasons for planning to earn a college degree. Since most parents share this perspective, we can only assume that parents have either told their children that this is the primary reason for going to college or that, at the very least, parents agree with and reinforce their children's views.

These findings suggest that interventions intended to influence the educational aspirations of students are most likely to succeed if they take place by the eighth or ninth grade. Beginning interventions that early does not ensure that students will go to college but is likely to keep college as a viable option in the minds of students and cause them to consider more carefully the courses they take in high school and the information they gather related to their postsecondary plans.

THE INFLUENCE OF FAMILY, FRIENDS, TEACHERS, AND COUNSELORS

Previous research on the effect of student background characteristics indicates that parental encouragement is the best predictor of postsecondary educational aspirations (Falsey and Haynes, 1984; Hearn, 1984; Sewell and Shah, 1978; Tillery, 1973). Using a variety of statistical techniques, we found that parents, other family members, and, to a lesser extent, peers had the largest effect on students' college aspirations (Shepard, Schmit, and Pugh, 1992). Descriptive and univariate analyses revealed that students in the ninth grade who talked the most with their parents (rather than with peers, teachers, or counselors) about their postsecondary plans were more likely to be planning to go to college and were also more likely to be certain of their plans. Our multivariate analyses consistently demonstrated that measures of parental support and encouragement to go to college were the best predictors of educational aspirations (Stage and Hossler, 1989; Hossler and Stage, 1992).

To further explore the impact of significant others (parents, siblings, and friends), we conducted multivariate analyses in which the variables included significant others, student achievement, and family background, specifically parental income and educational level; parental encouragement for their children to continue their education; students' achievement level (as measured by high school grade point average); frequency of students' discussion with peers, teachers, counselors, and others about their plans after high school; and students' involvement in high school activities.

The single most important predictor of postsecondary educational plans is the amount of encouragement and support parents give their children (Stage and Hossler, 1989). Parental encouragement was defined by frequency of discussions between parents and students about the parents' expectations, hopes, and dreams for their children. During our interviews, we asked students to think about materials they received in the mail from Indiana's statewide education information center (the Indiana Career and Postsecondary Advancement Center, or ICPAC). ICPAC mails four newsletters, a postsecondary planning folder, and two parent/student surveys to all students during their ninth-grade year. Students also receive two newsletters during each of their tenth-, eleventh-, and twelfth-grade years. Of all the materials, the students and parents remembered the surveys as being the most important material they received. One student remembered that answering the ninth-grade survey was the first time that he had had a detailed discussion with his parents about his plans after high school. "The survey got us talking so that we could answer the questions." This finding helped us understand the role of parents and how interventions might be devised to influence the college planning process.

Parental support, however, is a more tangible form of parental backing than parental encouragement. Parental support includes parents saving for postsecondary education, taking students on visits to college campuses, or attending a financial aid workshop with their child. Laura's parents and Michelle's mother talked more often to them about their expectations than did Allison's parents. Laura's, Sam's, and Seth's parents reported that they had started saving for the college expenses of their children.

In most of our statistical analyses, we had to remove the parental support variable to fully explore the extent to which other factors had an effect on the early postsecondary educational plans of students, although we do not suggest that parental support and encouragement is sufficient to determine students' plans. Other factors are necessary for students both to develop aspirations and to achieve their goals. As students moved closer to high school graduation, it became increasingly apparent that parental support and encouragement alone did not determine whether the students in our study actualized their plans to enroll in college.

We did not have survey data for students with siblings attending college. Nevetheless, interview data lead us to conclude that ninth-grade students with siblings or near family members who had attended or who were currently attending college were more likely to have college aspirations. These siblings and family members described their college experiences and extolled the benefits of getting a college education. Jerome and Laura had older siblings who were preparing to enroll in college. Other students in our interview subsample reported visiting older siblings at college or traveling with siblings who were visiting college campuses. Having an older sibling or parent currently enrolled in college exerts a strong influence on the educational planning of students, and from the interviews, we found that these opportunities to talk about education resulted in greater first-hand knowledge about college. Again, there was variation among students: Allison had an older sister who had graduated from a vocational school and who was currently enrolled in a university. Nevertheless, her sister's advice and example had no impact on Allison's aspirations in the ninth and tenth grades.

In examining the effects of peers on predisposition, we found that ninth-grade students with friends who planned to continue their educations after high school were more likely to have college plans. Other studies (Coleman, 1966; Falsey and Haynes, 1984; Russell, 1980; Tillery, 1973) reported that the more students come into contact with other students with college plans, the more likely they are to consider going on to college. The importance of peers in relation to such variables as parental encouragement and support and student achievement was small, but the relationships in several sets of analyses were consistently statistically significant.

In several analyses using multivariate techniques, we failed to find a significant relationship between students' educational aspirations and the amount they talked to teachers and counselors. In addition, our subsample of students never indicated that teachers or counselors had an impact on their predisposition to go to college.

THE EFFECT OF STUDENTS' BACKGROUND AND ACTIVITIES

Not surprisingly, as the grade point average of students increased, the likelihood that they planned to go to college after high school increased. Indeed, next to parental encouragement, student achievement (as measured by self-reported grade point average) was the best predictor of postsecondary aspirations (Shepard, Schmit, and Pugh, 1992). This finding is consistent with previous research (Bishop, 1977; Jackson, 1978; Sharp et al., 1996; Tuttle, 1981). Our research and that of others (McDonough, 1997; Weis, 1990) also suggested that students who earn better grades receive more encouragement from parents—and also from teachers, peers, and other family members—to continue their education. In addition, grades are an indicator of success, and success itself encourages continued involvement in the source of that success—school. Nevertheless, like parental encouragement, good grades alone are not sufficient, nor even a very good predictor, of a predisposition to go to college. For example, one student in the group of students we interviewed was an A-minus student who had been admitted into an honors program at Purdue University in November of his senior year. Yet, when we contacted him one year after high school graduation, he was living at home, had gotten married, and had gone into business with his stepfather.

We also examined the role of family income on predisposition. Previous reviews of research on the impact of family income on students' educational aspirations is mixed (Hossler, Braxton, and Coopersmith, 1989; Paulsen, 1990), and in the early stages of this study, we found that parental income was not a good predictor of the postsecondary educational plans of students (Hossler and Stage, 1992; Stage and Hossler, 1989). Bateman (1990) also found no statistically significant relation between parental income and students' educational plans. When we focus on the likelihood that students realize their aspirations, we find that parental income plays a significant role, but in the early stages of the college decision-making process, parental encouragement and support, along with good grades, are more important than family income. Thus, what parents do and say are more important than family wealth in the development of educational plans and aspirations.

Although parental income does not influence predisposition, parents' educational level does. As parental education level increases, children are more likely to plan to go to college (Hossler and Stage, 1992; Stage and Hossler, 1989). This finding is intuitive and is well supported by other research (Manski and Wise, 1983; Trent and Medsker, 1967; Yang, 1981). Parents with college educations are more likely to value education and to transmit their values to their children. In addition, analysis of our interview data demonstrates that parents who have gone to college are familiar with the experience and are better equipped to explain to their children how the college system is structured, how it works, and how the student can prepare for it.

Other background characteristics included in our analyses are ethnicity and gender. In their reviews of relevant research Hossler, Braxton, and Coopersmith (1989) and Paulsen (1990) reported that ethnicity and gender have little or no effect on the educational aspirations of students. No statistically significant differences in the educational aspirations of ninth-grade African American and Euro-American students were found (Bateman, 1990; Hossler and Stage, 1992). Interestingly, however, there are important differences by gender and ethnicity in the factors that influence educational aspirations.

In several sets of analysis using multivariate causal modeling techniques, female students consistently reported talking significantly more to their parents than did male students. However, they also reported talking more to their friends, teachers, and counselors about their plans. For male students, parental encouragement and support and student achievement explain most of their postsecondary plans. There were small, insignificant differences among African American and Euro-American female ninth-grade students but clear differences between females and males of both races. African American males were the most distinctive group in all of our analyses; using the variables from our models, we were repeatedly less successful in predicting or explaining the factors that influence the postsecondary aspirations of black male ninth-grade students.

Student involvement in student athletics, student government, other student clubs and organizations (ROTC, academic clubs), and external groups such as church youth groups is minimally significant. Students who are involved in more high school activities are more likely to have higher educational aspirations (Hossler and Stage, 1992; Stage and Hossler, 1989). This phenomenon has not received much attention in previous research (Hearn, 1984, reported similar results). Since we devoted little attention to this variable, we can only speculate as to the reasons for this finding. We believe the degree of student involvement in high school activities may be an indicator of overall levels of motivation and self-confidence among students.

The overall pattern of our results indicates that, in the ninth grade, parental encouragement, student achievement, and parental education, in that order, have the greatest influence upon students' college plans, parental encouragement and support far outstripping any other variable. As a result, efforts to influence students' college aspirations should focus on their parents. If parents cannot be influenced, then efforts to improve student academic performance might also have positive effects on students' college aspirations.[1]

THE INFORMATIONAL NEEDS OF STUDENTS

Through surveys administered to the sample (both students and their parents) in the ninth and tenth grades, we also explored the types of information needs of students and their parents. We wanted to learn more about the types

1. Several studies have found that characteristics of the high schools in which students are enrolled (such as the general income level of the surrounding community) and the academic track in which students are enrolled also influence the educational aspirations of students (Alexander et al., 1978; Hearn, 1984; McDonough, 1997; Sharp et al., 1996). Unfortunately, we did not include measures of these variables in our longitudinal study.

of information students and parents thought would be helpful during the predisposition stage.

Students were most interested in obtaining more information about career opportunities in areas related to their interest, college admissions requirements, and financial aid assistance. Interesting differences were evident between students and parents. Parents were much more interested in learning more about the costs of postsecondary education and the financial aid system than were students: 60 percent of the students and 77 percent of the parents wanted information about financial aid. Among the eight students highlighted in chapter 1, only Sam reported that he understood financial aid issues as early as the ninth grade.

SUMMARY AND CONCLUSIONS

Parents' expectations and encouragement have the greatest effect on the predisposition stage of the college decision-making process. This is followed by student achievement, parents' educational level, the influence of peers, and involvement of students in high school organizations and activities.

Parents encouragement and support for postsecondary education is a deciding factor for many students in the formation of their plans. By the time their children are in ninth grade, many parents already have specific questions about college and its costs. In addition, approximately 58 percent of female and 52 percent of male ninth-grade students in our sample reported thinking about their futures "constantly" or "a great deal." (This leaves, of course, a substantial percentage of ninth-grade students who did not think much about their post–high school plans.)

Our findings also show that the development of college plans vary by gender and race. Female ninth-grade students thought more about their plans and talked more to parents, peers, teachers, and counselors than did male students. We do not yet fully understand the sociological factors that influence African American male students. Given the current level of concern about this population, this topic clearly merits more research.

For parents, public policy makers, and institutional policy makers whose goal is to increase the number of students who hope to go to college, our research identifies several possible areas of intervention. Since parents play the decisive role in shaping the educational aspirations of their children, intervention should be focused upon parents. These interventions need to start early, since most students formulate their plans by the eighth or ninth grade. This suggests that intervention programs must reach parents before their children reach the eighth grade. Longitudinal studies of children demonstrate that the effects of families and schooling are cumulative (Alexander et al., 1978; Coleman, 1966; Rumberger, 1982). Thus, intervention needs to have started by the time students enter fifth or sixth grade.

Our findings reveal that by the ninth grade parents are already interested in financial aid. In addition, most parents and their children identify getting a good job as the most important reason for going to college. This implies that interventions targeted at parents should focus on the connections between a college education and the labor market. In addition, intervention programs should provide information about college costs and student financial aid. Efforts to help families engage in early financial planning for college are important. In later chapters, we show that students view any effort on the part of parents to save for the students' education as a strong and tangible form of support. More important than the amount of money saved is the fact that parents are saving.

In addition, we speculate that, at this point in the process, the information on financial aid and college costs should be simple. Parents are not likely to be interested in the details of Pell grants or state scholarship programs or in college payment options. At this early stage in the decision-making process, parents and students simply need to know that financial aid is available to help qualified students attend college. Parents should be constantly reminded that the tuition at most colleges and universities is not $30,000 a year. Early information on college costs and financial aid should be designed to reassure families that college is an affordable and viable option for qualified students.

Intervention efforts should focus upon getting parents and students to talk about students' futures. Parents need to articulate their educational expectations for their children. Intervention programs should also focus on activities that bring peers together to discuss their college plans and aspirations. Special attention may need to be given to African American males, because the factors that influence their educational aspirations are less certain. Intensive, longitudinal, ethnographic studies, like the work of McDonough (1997), are essential if we are to come to an understanding of the experiences and social factors that influence the educational aspirations of African American male students.

The lack of any relation between teacher and counselor support and college aspirations is intriguing. In recent years, Boyer (1987) and Orfield and Paul (1993) have called for improved high school counseling and guidance as a means to increase the college-going rates and to make the transition from high school to college smoother. The lack of a relationship leads to interesting speculations. Is it because counselors do not interact enough with students? However, it is also possible that most students simply do not look for and are not ready to receive information and encouragement from teachers and counselors in the eighth or ninth grade. We explore these issues in greater detail in subsequent chapters.

McDonough's work in this area (1994, 1997) reported that guidance counselors at private high schools do have a strong influence upon the college destinations of students. These private high schools have much smaller student-to-counselor ratios, and there is a great deal more emphasis upon college guidance. Perhaps, counselors and teachers could have more impact on students. However, untangling the impact of counselors and teachers upon the postsecondary plans of students enrolled in private high schools is complicated, because their parents usually have higher levels of education and family income and give their children a great deal of support and encouragement.

In contrast, some of our results (reported in later chapters) suggests that ninth-grade students focus on internal sources of support and information, such as parents and siblings. By the time students are in the eleventh and twelfth grades, they shift toward external sources of support and information, such as teachers, counselors, peers, and admissions counselors. Perhaps a greater investment in counseling in junior high school and the early years of high school could raise the aspirations of many students. It is also possible, however, that most seventh-, eighth-, ninth-, and tenth-grade students are not developmentally ready to seek or receive information from individuals outside the family. This is an intriguing area for research and for intervention programs that could be monitored and evaluated.

In part 2 of this book, we examine the students of our total sample when they were high school sophomores and juniors. We also explore in depth the plans and concerns of Allison, Amy, Jerome, Laura, Sam, Seth, Michelle, and Todd. Our research questions center on the impact of parents, student ability, peers, teachers and counselors, and college information on the postsecondary plans of students in our sample. We also continue to track the chronological development of students' plans. We are particulary interested in when students are ready for certain types of information and intervention and when they refine their decisions about their postsecondary educational plans.

PART TWO

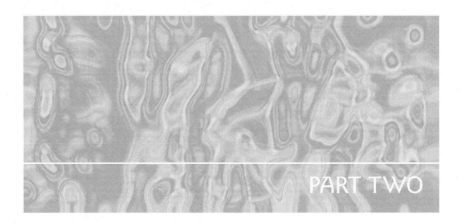

Searching for College Opportunities

In part 2 we consider a less-examined but important stage of the college decision-making process: how students search for colleges. During the sophomore and junior years, students begin to seriously examine possible postsecondary schools to attend and are also discovering what characteristics are important to them. It is a complex process; as they learn more about the schools they are considering, they discover questions about schools they have not considered. As they develop new criteria for schools, they alter the list of schools they are considering. In chapters 3 and 4, we examine how the search process unfolds and the factors that influence this stage of college decision making.

3

Looking Ahead

In this chapter, we examine how the postsecondary plans of Allison, Amy, Jerome, Laura, Sam, Seth, Michelle, and Todd continued to evolve during their sophomore and junior years in high school. During the tenth and eleventh grades, Sam, Michelle, and Seth began to think seriously about their postsecondary educational plans. They were specific about their plans but were also simultaneously exploring other options. Life after high school no longer seemed so far away. Jerome and Laura were also thinking more about their postsecondary educational plans, but they shifted between certainty and uncertainty about their plans.

During the search stage of the college decision-making process, some students in our study had still not decided whether or not to continue their education after high school and were searching among educational and noneducational alternatives. Most of the students in our study were trying to determine what college characteristics were important to them and, simultaneously, searching for colleges to consider attending. Allison and Amy, although they were thinking about their future plans, remained less focused than the other students. Amy never mentioned the possibility of postsecondary education. Allison sometimes voiced thoughts about attending a vocational or technical school, but these thoughts always sounded more like wishful thinking than serious planning. At the other end of the continuum, Sam was already actively considering particular colleges.

In the discussions that follow, we focus upon several factors: the influence of parents, peers, teachers, and others upon the postsecondary plans of the eight students during their sophomore and junior years; the similarity of these career and educational plans to these students' plans in the ninth grade; the costs of postsecondary education and student financial aid; and how students identified the specific colleges they might attend.

As part of this focus, we also look at how the admissions marketing material sent by colleges influenced the which colleges were considered by these students and also explored their (and their parents') knowledge of financial aid. Students and parents were asked to estimate the tuition expenses of a low, moderate, and high-cost college. They were also asked to estimate the room and board expenses at a low, moderate, and high-cost college. Since we knew which institutions these students were considering attending, we could judge the accuracy of their estimates. We also asked students and parents whether they thought they would be eligible for financial aid—and how much.

Allison

The strongest image of Allison among research team members was of a young woman without much direction, self-confidence, or ambition. During her sophomore year, Allison's mother told us that, as far as she knew, Allison had no plans for what she would do after high school. Her pattern of uncertainty was a continuation of the pattern during her first year in high school, and it persisted into her junior year.

In her sophomore year, Allison said that her sister was continuing to encourage her to go to a four-year college or to Ivy Tech State College after she graduated. However, Allison indicated that she would probably "just get a job and live somewhere around here" after she finished high school. During our first interview with Allison in the fall of her junior year, she said that she would probably work right after she finished high school but that, eventually, she would earn a vocational degree from Ivy Tech State College. She had no specific career plans or goals. Her mother was encouraging her to consider entering military service, since she had no other goal in mind.

The information from Allison and her mother about Allison's postsecondary plans was more contradictory than from any other student or parent in our study. In Allison's junior year, her mother told us that she had suggested many possibilities for Allison's future. Allison, however, told us that she had not received any encouragement from her parents regarding her postsecondary plans. Indeed, in December she reported that she had not talked at all to her parents about her plans. Although, at one point during her junior year Allison told us she had spent a great deal of time exploring her postsecondary options, her mother indicated that Allison had not started to think about her plans until very recently. Furthermore, her mother said that Allison had done nothing to explore her options. Both Allison and her mother reported that, while a few of Allison's friends planned to attend a college after high school, most planned to stay in the area and work.

In December, Allison told us that she had a friend who was going to attend Ancilla College and that she too was considering attending Ancilla. However, by March she had not contacted or investigated Ancilla or any other college. When we asked her if she planned to visit Ancilla that year, she responded, "No, it's too far from home."

During an interview in May of her junior year, Allison reported that she had been thinking more about her postsecondary plans and had decided that she wanted to be an auto mechanic. When we asked her why she was interested in this field, she responded, "I helped my father work on his car a couple of weeks ago and really enjoyed it." Her parents were surprised; in fact, her mother later told us that her husband did not even recall this incident. Nevertheless, her mother was delighted to have Allison express an interest in any field. She encouraged Allison to work at her brother-in-law's gas station to see if she would like this kind of work. However, Allison did not follow up on this suggestion.

We asked Allison if she had received college marketing materials through the mail and if she had been contacted by any colleges. She told us that she had begun to receive information during the spring of her junior year and that she had read it as soon as it arrived. Allison's mother had asked one of Allison's sisters to arrange for Allison to get information about programs at Lincoln Tech, a nearby vocational institute. In addition, Allison wrote to a correspondence school after seeing a course on auto mechanics advertised on television. Overall, however, there was little evidence that marketing activities and postsecondary information had any impact on Allison's postsecondary education plans.

Allison's knowledge of college costs proved to be limited and inaccurate. She overestimated the costs of attending all types of postsecondary educational institutions. Allison also told us that the cost of a college education would be "very important if I decided to go." Allison's postsecondary plans and aspirations proved consistent with the picture of her that emerged during her ninth-grade year. She lacked a commitment to both postsecondary education and a career after high school. By the end of her junior year, we began using Allison's statements to develop a metaphor for her aspirations and plans. Indeed, this became a metaphor for a subset of students in our study whose plans vacillated and who seemed uncertain about their goals throughout high school. Allison told us that Ancilla College was "too far" from her home for her to visit the campus; in fact, Ancilla is approximately two hours from her home. In many ways, making any type of postsecondary plan was "too far." Increasingly, with respect to her postsecondary aspirations, it seemed that Allison "did not know how to get there from here."

In her sophomore year, Amy continued to report that she was living with her mother, although we often wondered whether her mother was really at home and, if so, how much support she was providing for Amy. Amy said that she was planning to enter military service after high school.

In our first interview with Amy during her junior year, we discovered several indicators that life was beginning to unravel for her. Her high school guidance counselor confided that he was worried about Amy, that she had already missed several days of school and that, furthermore, he did not think Amy was living at home with her mother. Indeed, he was not even sure that Amy's mother had a place to live at the moment.

Amy volunteered to us that she was not living at home but with her older sister. Amy's sister, her husband, and their two children lived in an apartment in Indianapolis. Amy slept on the sofa in the living room. Amy's anger and despair were palpable. She once again told us that she wanted to enter military service as soon as she could after high school, that she wanted to get as far away from Indianapolis and her mother as possible. "I don't know if I will ever come back here." Amy had applied for the ROTC unit at her high school but was not sure that she would get in because of her grades. At the time of our first interview, getting into the ROTC appeared to be the most important goal in Amy's life; she thought that it would ensure that she would get into military service after she graduated from high school.

Amy did not come to school on the date we were supposed to conduct our second interview, in December. The home phone number she had given us had been disconnected. We sent her a letter to her home address, asking her to make a collect phone call to one of us at home in the evenings. In January of her junior year, she made the collect call, from a telephone booth, "not too far from where her sister was living," she said. Amy told us that she was still living with her sister but that her sister's phone had been disconnected and that she would probably be moving from her sister's soon because things were just too tough for her sister and her husband. We asked if she would move back in with her mother. Amy said no, that she was not sure where her mother was and that, in any case, she would not go back to her mother's. Amy did have some good news; she had gotten into the army ROTC at her high school. She felt very good about this; the pride in her voice was evident.

Unfortunately, this was our last contact with Amy. She did not attend any of our scheduled interviews. Despite our efforts to reach her by mail and our asking her to place collect telephone calls to us, she never called. The high school counselor was not free to give any details on Amy. Part of this was because of legal restrictions on him, but we also believe that he did not know a great deal about what happened to Amy. We do know that she finished her junior year, but she did not re-enroll for her senior year. As far as we know, she never graduated from high school. No other student in our interview subsample had a more difficult family situation or less family support. Perhaps because of her difficult situation, Amy had a clearer vision of what she wanted to do than many of our students. She may have succeeded in joining the military; however, the armed services requires a high school diploma or the GED. At any rate, we hope Amy eventually got where she wanted to go.

Jerome

During the time that Jerome was enrolled in the tenth and eleventh grades he changed both his educational and his vocational aspirations several times. Although he continued to plan to earn a four-year college degree, for a brief period of time when he was a junior he talked about working for one or two years before entering college. His career interests shifted among law, law enforcement, fire fighting, business management, and dentistry. Throughout these two years, his mother expressed concern about the effort Jerome put into his school work. About his work in the tenth grade, his mother commented, "He is going to have to do something and start using his brain."

In his sophomore and junior years, Jerome continued to report that he was receiving strong encouragement from his parents to attend a four-year college after high school, that his parents constantly told him that, with respect to college, "I can do whatever I want." His father wanted Jerome to go to college and not end up working in the shop, as he did. Jerome's mother said, "My husband tries to help Jerome with his work, but they don't necessarily want help." By his junior year in high school, Jerome's grades had fallen; he was now earning mostly C's.

Jerome consistently reported that he talked more to his friends than to his parents about his postsecondary plans. In Jerome's case, his peers may not have been a positive influence, since many of his friends did not plan any form of postsecondary education. His mother once commented, "His friends are not of a college nature," and this worried her.

Starting in the sophomore year, Jerome had considerable exposure to higher education. His brother was a first-year student at Indiana University in the fall of Jerome's sophomore year. During the next three years, Jerome made several visits to Indiana University to visit his brother, and this gave him a great deal of information about the college experience. But his older brother also cast a long shadow over Jerome. Reflecting on his brother's role in his life, Jerome said, "People expect me to be just like him. When he was here he was the president of the student council and the vice president of the Indianapolis YMCA Youth Council. Everywhere he goes, he just seems to know a lot of people. Everybody expects me to be just like him. I am just a small, little junior."

During Jerome's sophomore year, he consistently indicated that he wanted to be a lawyer or a police officer. In the fall of his junior year, Jerome told us that he had been thinking about becoming a firefighter immediately after high school. He investigated this career, however, and learned that he would have to be twenty-one years old to join and decided he did not want to "sit around for three years." In March of that year, he told us he wanted to go into either criminology or business management. Later in the same interview, he said, "I used to change so often, but I have stuck with criminology for a while now. I wouldn't mind doing undercover work. Business management, though, I don't really think I would like that much." In his last interview, he said he was thinking about studying law or becoming a dentist but that he was still interested in criminology.

Although Jerome was uncertain about his career plans, he was actively gathering information to help him make decisions. In addition to information about careers and majors, he was gathering information about colleges and talking to his counselor about college. In the spring, Jerome reported he was regularly receiving college information in the mail. Unlike some of the students in the sample who told us they put the information aside to read later, Jerome said, "When colleges send me stuff, I look it over to see if they have criminology programs. Most places have business. . . . I've been looking at that."

Although Jerome was still uncertain about many aspects of his aspirations, he was taking active steps to investigate his options and prepare for college. He took the PSAT early in the eleventh grade. He had already talked to his counselor about what colleges he should consider and where to look for scholarships. He also continued to participate in the minority engineering program. As noted, when he was interested in fire fighting he gathered sufficient information to decide that he did not want to be a firefighter. In May he was also enrolled in a course to prepare him for taking the SAT. All of these are indicators that Jerome did not passively wait, like Allison, to have information provided to him by others.

As a sophomore, Jerome was primarily interested in attending Ball State University or Indiana University. In the fall of his junior year, he had expanded the list to include Vincennes University (the only public two-year community college in Indiana, which is also a residential campus). By December, Jerome was talking more to his guidance counselor. He was also receiving admissions material from out-of-state colleges, but his parents strongly opposed his attending a college out of state. On several occasions, his mother had mentioned that "there are plenty of good public colleges right here in Indiana, where he can get a good education and not have to pay so much money." Jerome's counselor had told him about a generous scholarship program for African American students at DePauw University (a selective liberal arts college in Greencastle, Indiana). Jerome seemed interested in learning more about the DePauw scholarships.

Jerome was reasonably knowledgeable about tuition costs and financial aid. In an interview in which we focused on college costs and aid, he successfully discriminated among low-, moderate-, and high-cost institutions. Although his brother had not qualified for financial aid, Jerome thought he might because his older brother and sister would still be in college at the time he was enrolled. He had thought about loans, although his parents were opposed to them. Jerome repeated his mother's views: "My mom always says, we pay cash on the line." But he believed that, with three kids in college, college costs and financial aid would be an important factor.

In our final interview of his junior year, in May, Jerome told us that he would be making a formal visit to Indiana University soon. His mother, though, reported that Jerome was grounded for getting low grades in some classes. His aspirations and his efforts to plan for college were somewhat paradoxical. His uncertainty about his major and even whether he would start college immediately after high school were characteristic of students in our study who were unlikely to attend college. However, the effort he was investing in learning about colleges and careers was characteristic of students who had high aspirations and who were likely to enter college immediately after high school.

Previous research had found that African American high school students reported higher educational aspirations than other students (Brown, 1982). In addition, the African American ninth-grade students in our total sample thought more about their postsecondary plans than did the Euro-American students in our sample. Yet, Indiana state-level data showed that proportionately fewer African American students than Euro-American students actually attended postsecondary educational institutions each year. In this last interview, we explained these findings to Jerome and asked him if he had any thoughts about these contradictions. His response was insightful. "Because of the stereotype, you know. To try to get out of the stereotype. We know that fewer of us go on to college, and we don't want to be part of that image. We don't take going as a sure thing. Probably we need it to get ahead."

Laura

In the ninth grade, Laura was already giving more thought to her postsecondary plans than many of her peers. However, during her sophomore and junior years, her plans and activities became more contradictory. She no longer seemed as certain or as focused, and an intriguing relationship between Laura and her parents became evident. By the tenth grade, Laura was no longer certain what she would do after she graduated; she was not sure of her major and not even sure she would enter a college or university immediately after graduation.

In the tenth grade, most of the students in our sample who planned to continue their education after high school talked primarily to their parents about their educational plans. Laura, however, like Jerome, talked more to friends than to her parents. Most of her information about colleges came from sources other than parents or family members. Interestingly, her parents reported that Laura talked mostly to them about her plans. In trying to gauge the impact of her friends, we asked her if most of her friends planned to go to college after graduation. She answered that some of her friends did plan to continue their education but that many were either undecided or did not want to go to college.

In her sophomore year, Laura was still specific about what she was looking for in a college, if she went. She was interested in small colleges (less than five thousand students) that offered many social activities. She was also interested in colleges that had a good record of job placement. Given that her sister was attending a university (DePauw), Laura was also concerned about college costs. In a spring interview, her parents said they would not even apply for financial aid for Laura because of the experience they had had with their older daughter. "The hassle of completing the forms was a waste of time," they said.

In the fall of her junior year, Laura's plans had again become more certain. She once again planned to attend a four-year college, though she was still undecided about her major. Early in the eleventh grade, she told us that she enjoyed reading mysteries and thought she might like police detective work and also that she was thinking about attending a police academy camp at Vincennes University during the coming summer. On another occasion she told us that she was thinking about becoming a legal secretary. When we asked why, she said, "It's something I could do instead of having to learn. I liked the stenography class I took. I could work for a real high-up lawyer."

The statement about working instead of having to learn is revealing. Laura was earning B's and C's in her junior year; but in comparison with her sister (who had been an excellent student), Laura did not think she was a good student. Indeed, she made statements about this often; and she seemed much more interested in her cheerleading activities and other school social programs than in her schoolwork. In addition, her parents provided frequent and blunt feedback about her lack of success as a student, and they narrowed her choice of schools by telling her that she could not get into several schools in which she was interested. "Laura was interested in Hanover College," her father told us, "but I told her she would never get in there with her grades."

During her junior year, Laura started to investigate career and college options. She talked to a high school counselor about majors and possible colleges to attend and picked up information about colleges from the counselor's office. Laura did not take the SAT until May of her junior year, so she was not inundated with mailings from colleges and universities. Nevertheless, she was receiving some mail from colleges, and she read these materials soon after she received them. In addition, both Laura and her father started sending away for information about colleges. We thought it was unusual for Laura's father to be doing this for her.

During her junior year, Laura considered a wide range of institutions. She expressed interest in a proprietary school, Indiana Business College, but also Hanover College, Ball State University, Purdue University, Indiana University at Bloomington, Moorehead State University (located in Kentucky), and some junior colleges in Illinois. Laura mentioned her interest in Indiana Business College to her father, but he said that this would not be good for her. "I don't think he will let me go. I don't really want to, anyway." We asked her why she was interested in Moorehead State University, which she had not mentioned before. She responded, "I don't know. My dad wants me to go there. He also wants me to look at junior colleges."

She told us, "My parents talk about college all the time with me. I have told them I like DePauw, but they said that with my grades I would never get in." We asked her to identify other colleges in which she was interested. She mentioned Hanover College, Augustana College in Illinois, and Indiana University at Bloomington. Since she had not taken the SAT, and thus was not likely to be receiving college admissions mailings, we asked her how she had become aware of these schools. Laura explained that she had visited Hanover College and Indiana University with her older sister when her sister was making her college visits. Laura had received a mailing from Augustana College, which was how she had become interested in that school. When we asked her what she liked about Augustana, she answered that it was small and that it was a long distance from home.

In her second interview, in the spring, Laura reported to us that she would be taking the SAT soon. We asked again what schools she was considering.

She told us she had eliminated Hanover from consideration because it did not offer a major in criminal justice and that she had added the University of Evansville. She had also added Ball State and Indiana State University because her parents thought she might not be admitted to Evansville and that Ball State and Indiana State University were good schools, close to home, and not difficult to get into. With a modicum of sarcasm she told us that she had added the University of Evansville to the list of schools she was considering because "my mother and father went there, and they told me I should take a look at this school."

Laura had received information from only a few schools. She did not know how the schools knew to send information to her, since she had not requested any. She noted that she read the material she was receiving. Her father had made her sit down and write letters of interest to Ball State, Indiana University–Purdue University at Indianapolis (IUPUI), and the University of Evansville. She had also filled out cards to receive more information about Indiana State University and Augustana College. In addition, Laura had talked to one of her teachers several times about her interest in criminal justice, and he had suggested that she seek out information about careers in criminal justice from her guidance counselor. Laura had followed up on this suggestion, had read the information, and had found it helpful. She now thought that being a private detective might not be realistic, but she was still interested in being a police officer.

We talked with Laura and her parents about the cost of higher education and about student financial aid. Laura told us that she did not know much about college costs but that she was aware that the University of Evansville would be "twice the cost of going to Ball State University and living on campus or three times the cost of living at home and going to the University of Southern Indiana." She reiterated, however, that she did not want to go to Evansville and also preferred not to live at home and go to college. When we asked her whether she thought she would be eligible for financial aid, she responded that she had not given college costs or financial aid much thought. Her parents had told her that they would pay for her college and that they made too much money to qualify for financial aid. She added that her parents often reminded her that if she had earned better grades she might have been able to get an academic scholarship, as her older sister had.

Laura's parents were well informed about the costs of attending various types of college. They were equally well informed about the federal and state financial aid system. Laura's father had taken out student loans when he was a student at the University of Evansville. He added that he probably would not apply for student financial aid for Laura. He had to fill out forms each year for Laura's sister to receive her academic scholarship, and every year, he said, he received a form letter saying that he and his wife were not eligible for need-based student aid.

During her junior year, Laura showed increased interest in her postsecondary plans. Her career plans seemed to be clearer, and she was considering some colleges. Her parents continued to play a major role; in fact, they were among the most directive of all the parents we interviewed. Laura at times voiced a desire to get "out from under" their guidance; but at other times she seemed content to let them make decisions and take actions for her. Laura made some effort to expand her sources of information beyond her parents by talking to her high school guidance counselor and reading some of the college admissions material she was receiving.

By the end of her junior year, our impression of Laura and where she was headed after high school had become much more complicated. She continued to engage in many of the more focused planning and information-gathering activities associated with students who had certain plans to go to college after graduation. However, her uncertainty about her plans and her major during her sophomore and junior years were not characteristic of most of the students with clear goals and aspirations. In addition, the role of her parents during these two years was different from any of the families in our interview subsample. They had high expectations and provided encouragement for Laura to continue her education but were simultaneously negative, discouraging, and overly involved in some aspects of her decision making. These contradictions made Laura and her family interesting subjects for our longitudinal study.

Sam

Sam's strong goal orientation continued to be evident throughout his sophomore and junior years in high school. In his sophomore year, his plans and aspirations were still very focused. He planned to attend a four-year college and earn a degree in science or engineering and to eventually earn a graduate degree. Sam took the PSAT during his sophomore year and engaged in other activities that were clearly designed to help him get ready to go to college.

In the tenth grade, Sam told us, "I learned about *Peterson's Guide* this fall, got it, and started reading it." He also talked to parents, friends, and teachers about his plans. Nevertheless, he credited his high school principal with providing the most information and exerting the greatest influence on his educational plans. He may have relied on the principal because neither of his parents had attended college.

As early as the tenth grade Sam was considering such elite institutions as California Institute of Technology (Cal Tech), Massachusetts Institute of

Technology (MIT), Purdue University, Rose-Hulman Institute of Technology, and the Purdue Engineering School located at Indiana University–Purdue University at Indianapolis (IUPUI). Sam's parents continued to provide high levels of support and encouragement. They told us that they expected to pay between $8,000 and $10,000 in annual tuition for Sam. This is a large commitment, especially since Sam was a strong student who might anticipate receiving merit-based financial aid from some less prestigious college or university. A willingness to pay such high levels of tuition is a concrete sign of parental support and encouragement.

In the summer between his sophomore and junior years, Sam's parents had taken Sam on a college tour. On one long trip they had visited MIT, Carnegie-Mellon University, Case Western Reserve University, and General Motors Institute (GMI). In addition, they had visited two engineering schools in Indiana, Purdue and Rose-Hulman.

Sam had an A grade point average and was ranked third in his class at the start of his junior year. All of his friends were planning to attend college. We asked Sam if his parents had ever told him they wanted him to go to college or what college they wanted him to attend. He responded, "Nope, they have never told me anything."

In earlier interviews he had not mentioned GMI or Case Western Reserve, but he had received information from a number of schools during his sophomore year. When we pointed out that, except for Purdue, all the schools he mentioned were private, he responded, "I think I like the more personal emphasis I sensed at the private schools I visited. Purdue seemed pretty large and impersonal when we went there. I felt like a number." He could not recall all of the schools he had heard from, but they included the University of Michigan, Northwestern University, the University of Miami, Georgia Institute of Technology, and West Point. We assumed he had been placed on the mailing lists of engineering schools as the result of his PSAT scores. Sam had not read all the material but only that from schools with either good engineering programs or other interesting programs.

Sam mentioned that he might visit Wabash College, a small, private, liberal arts college located in Indiana. One of Sam's best friends was probably going to Wabash, and Sam noted that it had a program that allowed Wabash students to transfer to Washington University in St. Louis to complete a degree in engineering. In addition, Sam's high school guidance counselor had suggested that he look at Wabash because "it had a very large endowment and a generous scholarship program."

In our second interview with Sam during his junior year, he discussed his visit to Wabash. He had liked the college and said he was seriously considering it. A member of the admissions office had told Sam that with his SAT scores and grades he could receive a large academic scholarship, even though his financial aid need analysis might show that he did not qualify for need-based aid. Sam commented that, since he was not likely to qualify for a need-based grant, he should consider Wabash because of its scholarship program. We pointed out that he might qualify for merit-based financial aid at other schools. "I know that" he answered, "but I also liked the feel of Wabash."

During our second interview, in the spring, Sam told us that he was no longer considering MIT, Case Western Reserve, or GMI, either because he was not interested in the focus of their engineering programs or because he thought he might not be admitted. He was going to apply to Purdue (because it was close to home, even though he did not think he would go there), Rose-Hulman, Wabash, and, Carnegie-Mellon. Except for Carnegie-Mellon, all of these schools were relatively close to home. Sam's interest in living close to home and family proved to be an interesting factor in his decision making. Sam also shared with us that if he went to a small college like Wabash or Rose-Hulman, he might be able to keep playing tennis, observing that he was not good enough to play at a larger university.

Sam's school career continued to go very well throughout the year. He now ranked second in his class. Sam's parents attended both parent interviews during Sam's junior year and were almost as excited about Sam's educational opportunities as Sam was. We had the sense that Sam's success in high school was an opportunity for them to experience vicariously things that circumstances had prevented them from doing. We talked about the schools Sam was considering throughout the year. Sam and his parents obviously talked frequently, because his parents were very knowledgeable about the details of his plans. In the spring, during our second interview, they were concerned that Sam was thinking too much about the scholarship at Wabash. They wanted him to choose the college that would provide him the best opportunities and did not want him to be influenced by tuition costs or financial aid. Sam's parents were not opposed to scholarships; they just did not want them to play a central role in his choice.

We explored Sam's, and his parents, knowledge of college costs and their eligibility for student financial aid. Given Sam's early interest in going to college and his parents strong support, we were not surprised that he understood the costs of going to college in detail, as did his parents. His father and mother had both attended financial aid workshops and estimated that they would not be eligible for need-based financial aid if Sam went to a public college. They reasoned that both of them had jobs, they had a savings account for Sam's education, and Sam was an only child, which meant that they had a low level of financial need. Sam and his parents believed that if he went to a private university he might be eligible for need-based student loans, but they were not even sure of this.

In his junior year, Sam continued to be the most goal-oriented student we interviewed. He also had the most detailed knowledge about colleges and their costs. He had added and deleted institutions from the list of colleges he was considering. Purdue and Rose-Hulman were listed all three years, but otherwise considerable variation was evident. Throughout this time period, his parents gave him a large amount of support, but he also started to rely more on information from outside the family, consulting with friends, high school personnel, and college admissions personnel.

Seth

In the ninth grade, Seth did not think much about his plans after high school, but by the time he was in tenth grade, he had started to think about his future. According to Seth, his grade point average was a solid B. He was still involved in high school activities, and though he still planned to earn a vocational degree after graduation, he was no longer as certain as he had been during his first year of high school. In Seth's case, the uncertainty was the result of rising aspirations rather than declining ones.

Seth described his parents as supportive of his educational aspirations, but neither they nor Seth said that they were strongly encouraging him to continue his formal education after high school. Most of his friends planned to attend a four-year college or university after high school, but in his sophomore and junior years, Seth continued to take classes in the vocational track. He hoped to become an auto mechanic or a carpenter. As a first-year student, Seth talked primarily to his parents about his plans, but during the next two years he was talking more to his counselors and teachers than to his parents. Seth's building trades teacher had been especially helpful and influential. In addition, his parents were willing to spend $4,000 to $6,000 annually for Seth's vocational degree. They hoped to have some financial aid but did not expect large amounts.

Seth hoped to attend a small vocational school (fewer than five thousand students). He planned to commute, but he also hoped the school would offer many activities in which he could become involved. He noted that low costs would also be very important. Although Seth was interested in a vocational education, the schools he was considering included a proprietary school and both two-year and four-year institutions: Indiana University–Purdue University at Fort Wayne, Ivy Tech State College at Fort Wayne, Vincennes University (a residential two-year college), and Indiana Institute of

Technology. He had also received unsolicited mail from local private four-year colleges, including Manchester College, Goshen College, and Tri-State University.

By the end of Seth's junior year, he was considering attending a four-year institution but still planned to pursue a short-term vocational degree in carpentry or auto mechanics. These considerations, of course, were not consistent. He had made some effort to read about building trades and to visit some construction sites, but he had not visited any campuses and had no plans to at the end of his junior year. Nevertheless, according to Seth's mother, he was beginning to consider other options. She attributed his changing educational interests to his participation in our study, saying that Seth was thinking more about his post–high school plans than he would have if he had not been part of our study. (After lengthy discussions students in our interview sample for whom participation was having an effect, we decided that our first concern was the students and not the results of our study. In a later chapter, we discuss the impacts of participation and offer programmatic interventions.)

Like each of the eight students highlighted, Seth had a complex and nonlinear educational evolution. The growing influence of teachers and counselors was, perhaps, not surprising, since neither of his parents had had college experience. Seth's high level of participation in school activities was not typical of students who did not plan to go on to college, nor was his large number of friends with college plans.

MICHELLE

Michelle's post–high school plans continued to focus on getting a college education. In the tenth and eleventh grades, however, she did not demonstrate the same degree of certainty that had been evident as a first-year high school student. Even though she still aspired to attend a four-year college after graduation, by the time she was a sophomore, Michelle was attending a regional vocational high school.

Michelle no longer indicated that she planned to earn a master's degree; a four-year college degree was the highest to which she now aspired. When we asked Michelle in her sophomore year why she wanted to go to college, she told us, "Times are getting hard. If you don't have an education past high school, you can't really get a good job, and I am a person who really loves to buy clothes." Michelle's mother continued to provide strong encouragement for Michelle's educational plans. Early in her sophomore year, Michelle began receiving information from Andrews University in southern Michigan, a school with ties to her church, but she was not seriously interested in Andrews.

As she entered her junior year, Michelle's uncertainty about her educational plans grew. She was now attending a vocational high school, earning mostly B and B-minus grades. Although she still wanted to earn a four-year college degree, early in her junior year she said she thought she might work for a while before entering college. Michelle's mother, while still supportive, did not think Michelle would earn a degree beyond a bachelor's degree.

Michelle did not know what most of her friends were planning to do after high school. "Most of my friends are tired of high school." Michelle had some career directions in mind, but she was still working through these issues. She tentatively planned to major in accounting and hoped for a high-status, well-paying job in which she would manage others.

Although Michelle appeared to be thinking more about which college she might attend, she had not done much to explore her options. As late as May of her junior year, the only college she knew much about was Andrews University. Her mother was encouraging Michelle to attend Andrews, but Michelle was not certain if this was what she wanted. She had been talking to her high school guidance counselors about career options but not about college options. She had written away for information about careers in accounting and banking. One of her classes had been taken to interview employees of a nearby bank.

In February, Michelle noted that she had been thinking about historically black colleges:

> *I read about a couple of them and talked to a friend about it. Somebody in his family went to an all black college, and I was like, yes, that's what I want. Then I thought about it and wondered if I was looking for the right thing. I really need a book that tells you about it or just start and call for information about them. I really haven't done that, so that's why I don't want to pinpoint that I am going to a black college. I have to know about the academics and the business department and all that stuff. . . . I have to start buckling down and getting in touch with different colleges, because I really don't know much about them.*

In May, Michelle told us, "the only college I have talked to is Andrews. I want to go to an all-black college in the South, but I just haven't talked to them or gotten any information yet." At the end of her junior year, Michelle had not written to any college or made any campus visits, nor did she have plans to do so. In addition to her lack of information about individual colleges, Michelle and her mother did not have much information about college costs or financial aid. Nevertheless, Michelle told us that financial aid would have a big impact on her decision because her family did not have much money.

During the course of her sophomore and junior years, Michelle's aspirations and plans developed in a pattern similar to those of Laura. She became less certain of her goals and aspirations. She lowered her educational expectations. Unlike Laura, however, who initiated explorations of her options (with help from her father), Michelle took few proactive steps to investigate her alternatives. Michelle did gather information about her career interests, but this did not motivate her to also learn more about college. She lacked important information about both college and college costs. She confided during her junior year, "I feel like I know what the outside of college is like but not the inside."

Todd

During his sophomore year, Todd's plans remained stable. While he reported that he continued to think about his post–high school plans a moderate amount, we saw no evidence of major changes in his plans. Since the ninth grade, Todd had planned to enlist in the marines, telling us that the marines were the most prestigious branch of the armed services. This plan was not surprising; Todd had two brothers in the marines.

Todd seemed satisfied with his plans and at the time was clearly excited about his future. Todd's parents were supportive of his plans. His father thought the military would offer Todd a good life. During his junior year, Todd's plans remained focused on his twin goals of joining the marines and hiking the Appalachian Trail, and he showed no interest in other career options. In the fall of his junior year, he was already planning some of the details of his hike and had identified camping places.

Todd continued to take classes in the general curriculum track at his high school: algebra, English, general science, world history, woodworking, auto mechanics. He was still earning mostly C's. Todd said he liked high school and believed that "everyone should at least finish high school. There are more possibilities out there than fast food for high school graduates."

Todd's mother told us that she and her husband had always supported Todd and encouraged him to pursue his goals, whatever they might be. "His father and I try to help him avoid mistakes we have already been through, but other than that, we let him make his own decisions." Todd's mother worried "a little" about all of her boys being in the marines but thought that it was a good and honorable career.

Todd's plans did not waver at all during his junior year. During his interview in the spring of his junior year, he told us that he had found a job cleaning up construction sites for a home construction firm. He said that the pay was good and that he was looking forward to the summer. Because Todd did not plan to go to college, we did not ask him or his parents questions about college costs and student financial aid. Although his goals were different, Todd's approach to his plans were similar to those of Seth: he formed clear aspirations at an early age, and he kept them through the first three years of high school.

SUMMARY

During their junior years in high school Jerome, Laura, Michelle, Sam, and Seth became more interested in planning what they would do after high school. However, only Sam's and Todd's educational and career plans remained stable. For Sam and his parents, their college visits and other activities put Sam in a good position to make sound decisions about his education. Sam's parents remained supportive of him and helped Sam make his decisions.

Jerome's parents and Laura's parents were knowledgeable about college and also had high expectations for their children. However, neither Jerome or Laura were dedicated to their studies. In both cases, the parents played dominant roles in setting boundaries on the educational options that Jerome and Laura were considering. Indeed, Laura's father appeared to be overly involved. Neither Jerome nor Laura appeared to have strong goals. Both vacillated about their goals and plans.

Michelle's goals and plans steadily eroded during her first three years in high school. She became uncertain whether she would even enter college immediately after high school. Although her mother provided support and encouragement, Michelle invested little time and energy in gathering information regarding her educational alternatives.

Seth's plans and aspirations appeared to be slowly expanding during his first three years in high school. In Seth's case, it is plausible that a constellation of factors, including support from teachers and counselors, a college-oriented peer group, high levels of high school involvement, and participation in this study, converged to cause him to reassess his post–high school plans.

Lack of goals, lack of a sense of self-efficacy, and lack of strong parental support and guidance left Allison without any clear goals and aspirations at the end of her junior year. In many ways, she fits the profiles of the students in our study who did not have college aspirations. Amy's presence in our study came to an end during her junior year. We never came to know her well enough to understand all of the factors that influenced her. Clearly, the lack of a stable home environment was a major impediment to the development of goals and aspirations.

Not all of the students who were not planning to go to college did so out of lack of direction or self-confidence. Todd demonstrated high levels of goal orientation and was confident of his future. Jerome, Laura, Sam, and Seth began to look beyond the family—to peers, high school teachers and counselors, work experience, college visits, and reading—for guidance.

For the students who were college bound (Jerome, Laura, and Sam), taking the PSAT or SAT exam was an important rite of passage for many reasons. The students viewed taking the SAT as an important step in their college plans. They attached importance to their performance and the impact their scores might have on their educational future. In addition, SAT scores become a trigger mechanism for receiving information about colleges. Laura, Michelle, and Seth did not take the SAT in their junior year, so they did not have access to as much information about colleges. For some students, admissions marketing material expanded their educational horizons.

Student and parental knowledge of the costs of postsecondary education and of student financial aid varied considerably. Jerome, Laura, and Sam, and their parents, were knowledgeable about colleges costs and student financial aid. In these families, both students and parents also seemed concerned about costs and financial aid. Michelle's and Seth's parents were not nearly as knowledgeable about these financial issues.

In the next chapter findings from several statistical studies based upon data from our surveys are discussed. These results extend our understanding of some of the issues that emerged from our eight students.

4

Factors in the Search Process

Throughout the time that the students in our study were high school sophomores and juniors, most of them were going through decision-making processes similar to those of the students in our smaller interview sample. As their high school years were drawing to a close, they were searching for postsecondary options and evaluating them. Some students, like Sam, were conducting this search process with more intensity than others; but most of them were at least beginning to consider their future alternatives.

Our insights into the decision-making process are derived from three sources. In addition to the junior-year interviews with the subsample of students described earlier, we carried out group interviews with a small number of students and parents during their sophomore year. These groups of students and parents were not followed in subsequent years, so we draw on these findings less. Nevertheless, their comments and experiences inform the results reported in this chapter. In addition, statistical analyses were conducted of the surveys that students and parents completed. By this time in our research, we were developing a large longitudinal data set, which permitted the exploration of a variety of analytical questions.

We summarize the results from our analyses and draw upon previous research to develop an understanding of the search stage of the college decision-making process. An analysis of students' decision making during the time they are in the tenth and eleventh grades is especially interesting because very few cross-sectional or longitudinal empirical studies of the educational decisions of this time period have been conducted. Thus, our research breaks new ground in examining these years.

During the sophomore and junior years, we shifted our focus from the formation of students' educational aspirations to the stability of their aspirations, of the types of college they were considering, and of the characteristics of these colleges that were important to them. We were interested in the following issues and questions:

1. How do the educational aspirations of students continue to develop and how stable are they? For example, to what extent do students sustain their aspirations during their sophomore and junior years. How many of the ninth-grade students who are undecided about their plans are still undecided as high school juniors?

2. How do students learn about college options and how do they evaluate them? What college characteristics, such as size, cost, distance from home, and academic reputation, are important?

3. What factors influence how students evaluate their college options? For students who plan to continue their education after high school, how do they decide which characteristics are important enough to cause one school to become an option and another school to be dropped from consideration?

4. Colleges spend millions of dollars each year to market themselves to students. What is the effect of these marketing efforts on high school students? How do students process this information and how does it influence the search stage of student college choice?

5. How knowledgeable are students and parents about college costs and student financial aid programs? How do their perceptions of college costs and student financial aid programs influence their educational aspirations?

6. Are there major themes that describe the role of parents in the college decision-making process? When do parents have the greatest influence in this process?

STABILITY OF PLANS

If parents, public policy makers, or institutions are to influence the educational plans of young people, we need to know more about the stability of students' plans and the factors that influence that stability.

Figure 4.1 displays students' post–high school plans in the ninth, tenth, and eleventh grades. Students' educational plans show a steady rise over time.

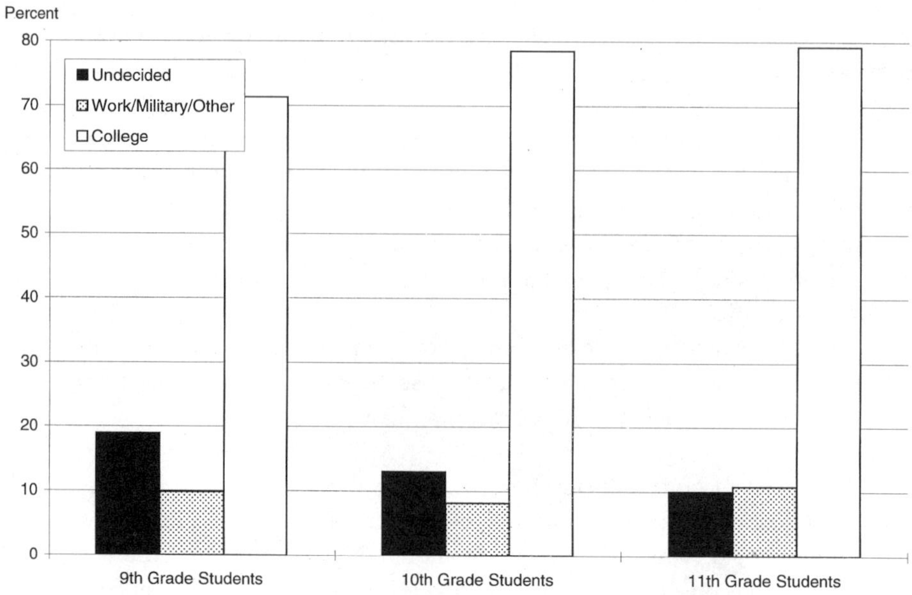

FIGURE 4.1 Students' Post–High School Aspirations in Ninth, Tenth, and Eleventh Grades

Among ninth-grade students, more than 70 percent planned to go to college; this figure for eleventh graders was 90 percent. The plans of students who were undecided in ninth grade became more certain over time. And the plans of ninth graders who planned to work, enter military service, or engage in other activities after high school changed by only a couple of percentage points.

Using multivariate statistical techniques, we found that sophomores who sustained their college plans reported talking more to their parents than to peers, teachers, or counselors about their plans. The results are similar to the findings for our subsample when they were in the ninth grade. We also found that sophomores with high grade point averages were more likely to plan to continue their education after high school.

These findings are similar to several other studies that looked at the aspirations of adolescents or the educational plans of high school seniors (Carpenter and Fleishman, 1987; Manski and Wise, 1983; and Zemsky and Oedel, 1983). For example, Conklin and Dailey (1981) found that the more parents talked to their children about their postsecondary plans, the higher their educational aspirations. Conklin and Dailey also found results similar to ours regarding the effects of student ability and family background upon students' educational aspirations.

CONSISTENCY AMONG COLLEGE CHOICES

Since the primary focus of our research was on students' paths to college, we asked all high school sophomores who said they planned to go to college to list up to five schools, in rank order, that they were considering (the consideration set; see Clark, 1993). We asked the same question when the students were juniors. Each institution was subsequently classified with respect to program (vocational or technical, two year, four year); control (public, private, proprietary); cost; admissions selectivity; and location (in state or out of state). We then looked at the stability of students' consideration sets and analyzed shifts in each student's first-choice institution.

Our analyses supported intuitive outcomes: few sophomores who planned to attend four-year institutions had shifted their preference to two-year institutions or to vocational schools by the time they were juniors. Although most students who planned to attend two-year schools or vocational schools sustained these plans, there was some shift toward four-year colleges. Seth illustrates this pattern. His plan as a first-year high school student was to get a job after high school. By his sophomore year, he was considering attending a two-year vocational school. By his junior year, he was contemplating attending a four-year college, though he still planned to earn a two-year vocational degree.

We also looked at shifts in specific institutions, comparing the top three institutions on each student's sophomore and junior consideration sets and found a high level of instability: 73 percent of the juniors did not list any of the same institutions among their top three choices that they had listed earlier. These findings suggest that between the sophomore and junior years most students are not certain of the specific college they might attend. This is not surprising. Jerome, Laura, and Michelle are good examples of this kind of instability, and they provide insights as to why their consideration sets were unstable. Laura was uncertain as to both her area of academic interest and where she might be admitted. As a result, she was doing a great deal of searching for schools and possible majors. Michelle's discussion of her possible interest in attending a historically black college, and her failure to gather information about this option, also helps explain her high level of instability. Jerome also expressed interest in several possible majors, and he was concerned about costs and financial aid. His parents made their views quite clear, but he was also getting advice from his high school counselor. Parental and counselor advice were not always consistent.

As anticipated, the consideration sets revealed stability with respect to cost and selectivity and a slight shift between the sophomore and junior years toward the inclusion of more private institutions. The costs of the schools being considered rose slightly. Overall, however, types of college remained stable. Again these findings are consistent with the pattern we found among our interview group. Sam primarily expressed interest in highly selective, private, engineering schools. Most of the schools in which Michelle expressed interest were small, private colleges. Jerome's consideration set consisted primarily of public institutions, and his parents strongly advised him in this direction. Only Laura's consideration set did not reflect this consistency; her consideration set included both public and private colleges. Students appeared to be exploring a range of institutions, but their explorations tended to be within a consistent set of public, private, or proprietary institutions.

CHANGING CHOICES

At the outset of our work, we hypothesized that as student ability increased their consideration sets would narrow. We reasoned that these students were more likely to come from families with college experience. We also hypothesized that these students would be more active in their search for colleges and, as a result, would develop well-thought-out consideration sets earlier than other students. We speculated that these students would start to eliminate less attractive or less realistic options earlier than other students, thus narrowing their consideration sets at an earlier point.

To test this hypothesis, we looked at whether the number of institutions in each student's consideration set was increasing, remaining the same, or getting smaller. In our first round of analyses, we simply counted the number of institutions on the list. Our assumption was that if the number of schools had decreased, students might be moving closer to making a final decision as to which college to attend. Between the sophomore and junior years, only 20 percent of the students in our sample narrowed their consideration sets. Indeed, the mean number of institutions being considered actually increased, from approximately two institutions to three. Although this increase in number of institutions is small, we call attention to this finding because later in this chapter we also report how the importance of college characteristics changed over time. These findings, and our discovery that the consideration sets of high school juniors actually increase in comparison with those of high school sophomores, suggest that the junior year is one of openness and discovery.

Using simple correlational statistics, we discovered that women were statistically more likely to consider a large number of schools. (The level of significance for all relationships discussed in this section was at the .05 level.) Students with higher grade point averages had larger consideration sets. Students considering more selective and more expensive colleges were also more likely to have large consideration sets. In addition, students with large consideration sets reported reading for pleasure more and studying more hours. Students who had narrowed their consideration sets by their junior year were more likely to come from families with low incomes and who had a father with a low educational level. We next employed a more rigorous set of analyses, using multivariate statistics; the same underlying relationship between the characteristics of students and their families and students' consideration sets were evident (Vesper, Hossler, and Bouse, 1991). In addition, high-ability students added and deleted more institutions from their consideration sets than did other students in our sample.

In our interview group, Sam best typifies these findings. Sam was near the top of his class. During his sophomore and junior years, he added and deleted several schools from his consideration set. General Motors Institute and Case Western Reserve University were not initially in his consideration set. However, by early in his junior year, they were on his list, and MIT and Cal Tech no longer appeared to be serious options. By the end of his junior year, Sam was considering Wabash College, an institution that does not even have an engineering program.

The general picture that emerges from these analyses is that students with higher grades and whose families have more education and higher incomes consider more colleges in their sophomore and junior years and are less likely to be narrowing their choices by the junior year. Students with larger consideration sets were also less concerned about college costs and more likely to be considering selective institutions.

These results demonstrate that our hypothesis was wrong. High-ability students with better-educated parents do not settle on a list of colleges early and then begin to narrow the list. In fact, quite the opposite is true. These findings are consistent with previous research on high school seniors that found that students with higher grades and who come from families with high levels of education and income apply to more schools, to more selective schools, and to more costly schools (Hossler, Braxton, and Coopersmith, 1989; Lewis and Morrison, 1975; Litten, 1982; Paulsen, 1990; Zemsky and Oedel, 1983). This study demonstrates that these trends are present in the sophomore and junior years.

We were fascinated with the complexity of the college decision-making process and elected to look at how stable students' ratings of the institutional characteristics were between their sophomore and junior years. The survey asked students to rate the following college characteristics: size of school, its distance from home, its cost, its academic reputation, whether it was private or public, whether it had a religious affiliation, the size of the community it was located in, and availability of financial aid. We used multivariate statistical techniques to explore whether the importance of these characteristics increased or decreased between the sophomore and junior years, thus measuring the specificity that students attached to college characteristics. We anticipated that students would identify an increasingly larger number of characteristics as either important or not important to them. In other words, we expected students to become more specific over time.

To our surprise, most high school juniors were less certain than they had been as sophomores with respect to the institutional characteristics. Although this was true for the majority of juniors in our sample, the trend was more pronounced as student ability increased: as student grade point average increased, the uncertainty about which college characteristics were important also increased. In addition, students who talked more to parents and family members than to peers and teachers were also less specific. But students who were actively engaged in learning more about college were more certain about college characteristics.

We were also interested in determining whether patterns were evident in the types of institution students were considering. Earlier in this chapter, we report that most students considered either public or private institutions during their sophomore and junior years. However, we asked a different question in this phase of our analysis, to determine if we could predict the types of college that students with similar characteristics were considering. For example, were students with low grade point averages and whose parents had lower levels of formal education more likely to be considering only public colleges?

We attempted to determine if the background characteristics could predict whether students were more likely to be considering small colleges, private colleges, or vocational schools; more expensive institutions; in-state or out-of-state schools; or more selective colleges. Surprisingly, background characteristics did not predict the types of college that students considered. Possibly, the limitation of our survey sample influenced these findings; Indiana is dominated by public institutions, and the two public flagship institutions, Indiana University and Purdue University, have high levels of recognition and enroll large numbers of in-state high school graduates. If this variability was reduced, statistically significant relationships are more unlikely.

Our best explanation for these results is that during their sophomore and junior years students are still discovering what to study after high school, what career they are interested in, and which educational institution will best meet their needs. As a result, their consideration sets contain a variety of institutions. A typical high school junior might be like Jerome, who during his junior year told us he was thinking about going to Indiana University (a major public research university), Vincennes University (a public residential two-year college), and DePauw University (a selective, in-state, four-year private liberal arts college). Consideration sets like this make it difficult for multivariate statistical techniques to find patterns between students' background characteristics and their educational plans.

The results of these analyses point to an interesting dynamic at work among tenth- and eleventh-grade students planning to go to college. By the tenth grade, most of the students in our sample had developed postsecondary plans and aspirations. Sophomores who aspired to continue their formal education had also developed lists of institutions they were considering attending. Sophomores also had a clearer idea than juniors of the institutional characteristics that were important in their decision-making process. During the junior year, students became less certain. We posit that as students move closer to high school graduation, questions about their postsecondary plans become more relevant. Juniors also spend more time learning about colleges, discovering questions they had not previously thought about. Recall Michelle's interview with us in which she reported a conversation with friends about historically black colleges. Up to that time, Michelle had not given much thought to these colleges. In subsequent conversations, Michelle had questions about these colleges and, as a result, grew more uncertain about her college options.

We speculate that many students go through processes like Michelle's. As high school juniors, they focus more attention on their futures. As they learn more about colleges, they uncover additional questions and additional college characteristics they had not thought about before. As a result, high school juniors become more uncertain about which characteristics are important to their decision making. Students who are originally undecided or who do not think they will continue their education after high school might go through a similar process. For some students, like Seth, as their educational aspirations increase they focus more energy on a wider range of educational options and become open to exploration.

Though high school juniors may eliminate some colleges from their consideration set, the total number of institutions being considered increases. This uncertainty is not unhealthy; it is part of a natural developmental process. Over time, as students become more accustomed to evaluating educational institutions, they also become better at processing the information they receive.

GATHERING INFORMATION

We were interested in the extent to which students gathered information about postsecondary educational institutions and how this information influenced their plans.

Schmit (1991) examined the information gathering, or search activities, of sophomore students in our sample and the effect of these activities on the students' educational plans. He identified three types of information gathering in the search stage: attentive search, active search, and interactive search. Attentive search is passive. Students do not actively seek information but are likely to pay attention to discussions about postsecondary education if the topic comes up. They may read material if it is mailed to them. Schmit described this as an "ear-to-the-ground" mentality. Active search, on the other hand, involves actively seeking out discussions about educational options. Interactive search includes student-initiated conversations with family members, with teachers and counselors, and with college admissions representatives. Interactive search also include sending for information and visiting campuses.

Using multivariate techniques, we examined the information-gathering activities of the sophomores in our sample. The results demonstrate that sophomores in an academic track in high school who reported talking to family members, peers, teachers, and counselors about their high school plans were likely to be engaged in active and interactive search. These student-centered variables, however, were strongly influenced by parental support and students' grade point average. Parents who reported high levels of support for their students' aspirations and who had made this support tangible by saving money for education had a strong positive effect on students' aspirations. Students with higher grades were also more likely to be in the academic track, talk more about their postsecondary plans, and think more about their plans. Students who earned higher grades also stimulated greater levels of parental support and saving; in the language of statistical analysis, we can say that higher student grade point averages had an indirect positive effect on the information gathering, or search activities, of high school sophomores.

Overall, however, Schmit did not find that many sophomores were actively searching for colleges. Our tenth-grade survey did not include questions about how frequently students received mailings from colleges, or the extent to which students were writing to colleges requesting information, or how often they visited college campuses. Students in the group interviews conducted in the sophomore year did not indicate they were engaged in these activities. Here again, we call attention to the interactive nature of our interviews and our survey research. The interviews were used to explore topics that emerged from our surveys. In addition, however, new themes and concerns that emerged from the interviews were also used to identify questions for inclusion in the next round of surveys. These observations are bolstered by the fact that the average number of schools that sophomores listed in their consideration sets was approximately two. Juniors, however, considered between three and four. From the perspective of both high school guidance counselors and college and university admissions staff, these results suggest that most sophomore students are not ready for detailed information about individual colleges. Instead, interventions targeted at sophomores should focus on educational aspirations and broad typologies of postsecondary institutions.

During the junior year, the search activities of the students in our study began to dramatically increase. By the middle of the second semester of the junior year, 43 percent of all respondents reported talking to friends, teachers, counselors, or parents about college. Another 61 percent had picked up information from high school counselors' offices or from local libraries. In addition, 55 percent sent off for information, and 55 percent visited one or more campuses. These findings indicate that the junior year is when students seriously begin to extensively gather information.

By their junior year, students were interested in information about specific colleges and universities. The number of institutions they considered increased and their search activities increased. In addition, students began to consult more with teachers and counselors, suggesting that, as students moved closer to high school graduation, school personnel played a more important role in helping students identify the colleges they should consider. By the end of the junior year, teachers and guidance counselors played an important role in assisting students learn about specific institutions. From the perspective of college policy makers, teachers and counselors may play an important role in helping students determine which specific schools to consider attending. By their junior year, students are shifting away from internal sources of information to external sources of information.

CONSIDERING THE COSTS

An area of significant change among both students and parents was in their knowledge of and interest in student financial aid and the costs of postsecondary education. In earlier years, parents were interested in information about costs, but they thought they did not know much about them or about student financial aid and their own eligibility for such aid. One student, when asked what she knew about the costs of college or her eligibility for student financial aid, responded, "Nothing. I have no idea." Students frequently told us that these issues were the responsibility of their parents, but by their junior year, they were much more interested in college costs and student financial aid. In addition, both students and their parents knew more about costs and student aid.

During their junior year, we asked each student from our subsample and one of his or her parents to estimate the costs of attending college for one year as a commuting student and as a residential student. We then compared their responses to the costs of colleges they were considering. We developed an index to assess the accuracy of these estimates (see appendix). The closer their estimates were to the actual costs of the institutions they were considering, the higher their accuracy rating (ratings were low, moderate, or high; students and parents who could not estimate college costs were assigned to a separate category). More than 60 percent of the students and parents were rated moderately or highly accurate, the students demonstrating a slightly better level of accuracy than their parents.

We also asked students the following three questions regarding student financial aid. Did they think they were eligible for financial aid? Why were they eligible (or ineligible)? And could they estimate how much financial aid they were eligible for? An index based upon their responses was used to rate students' knowledge about student financial aid. Students were rated as having knowledge levels of low, some, moderate, high, and very high. More than 83 percent of the subsample was rated as having moderate to high levels of knowledge of student financial aid. When in the students' junior year we asked students and parents whether they knew if they were eligible to receive financial aid, more than 90 percent reported that they did know. Despite the problems of self-reported information, this is a dramatic change from the responses of ninth-grade students and parents and from tenth-grade students in our sample. In these two previous years, most respondents said either that they lacked information about student aid or that they were not interested in information about student aid.

Overall, our results suggest that by the junior year students and parents are interested in and knowledgeable about college costs and student financial aid. This finding is consistent with those on information gathering. If students are actively engaged in information gathering, both they and their parents are likely to learn more about college costs and student financial aid. As noted, this move toward more information gathering and increased knowledge about college costs and financial aid are intuitive. Students are getting closer to the end of their high school years, and they need to have more information to make decisions.

THE PARENTAL ROLE

The impact of parental support and encouragement on student aspirations is significant. This is not surprising, since parents play an unquestioned role in the lives of their children and have a personal interest in seeing their children succeed. Substantial research on student's college choice indicates strong parental influence throughout the college-choice process (Galotti and Mark,

1994; Hossler, Braxton, and Coopersmith, 1989; Litten and Hall, 1989; Maguire and Lay, 1981). Much of our earlier work highlighted the importance of parental influence upon student college choice (Hamrick and Hossler, 1995; Hossler and Stage, 1992; Hossler and Maple, 1991).

As part of our study, we gathered data from a matched set of students and parents and, through surveys and interviews, gained a glimpse of the parent's role in the student college-choice process (Schmit and Hossler, 1995). This longitudinal perspective on the role of parents enabled us to develop a model on the parental role. We do not suggest that each student and parent exhibited every component of the model, but many themes were consistently found. We introduce the entire model at this point, since it appears to fit at this juncture in the book. We revisit the model in the concluding chapter, as we summarize the entire study. The components of parental involvement were categorized into parental influence, parental encouragement, and parental support.

Parental influence is best described as sending signals. Five types of signals emerged from the student and parent interviews: predisposition, direction setting, price, proximity, and quality. The predisposition signal includes parents', siblings', and other relatives' educational level. With the direction-setting signal, students know whether they are going to college long before high school and when in high school enroll in a particular curriculum, which sets the direction for their high school experience. The price signal was also strong in our study. The proximity signal influences whether students stay in state or go out of state for their college education. In our study, while parents encouraged students to explore out-of-state institutions, most hoped their students would stay in state. The quality signal, or academic reputation of the college, is also important, although parents and students may not know how to define it.

Parental encouragement has three components: attitude, consistency, and congruence. Parental attitude is reflected in the parents' desire to do "whatever makes them happy." Consistency means that parents are consistently encouraging throughout the choice process. Congruence means similarity between the plans of students and those of their parents.

Parental support can be described as action-oriented activities that support the student's search. Students appear to see evidence of parental support in such activities as saving and preparing for college. Savings activities include parental saving and student saving; preparation activities include visiting campuses, assisting in filling out forms (financial aid, applications, housing, scholarship), attending summer camps and programs, reviewing information, and job shadowing.

Parental involvement was an integral part of the decision-making process of every student in our study. During interviews with both students and parents, the parents were almost always more expressive than their children and were interested in finding ways to help their children make informed decisions. Parents' involvement spanned a range, from a father who did almost everything for his daughter, including enroll her in college, to a mother who said, "I just can't wait for him to get out of the house." Most parents were interested, concerned, and engaged in their children's plans.

The time frame when parents have the most influence on the college choice process appears to be in the earlier stages of the process. For some students, this time frame may begin at birth and then decrease as students enter high school. Many of the students profiled in this book felt the influence of their parents before the ninth grade, but this result is more impressionistic for the larger survey sample. Regardless of time frame, students' were influenced by their parents' signals.

Parental influence is strongest before high school. Once the student is on track, parental influence is less apparent. Parental encouragement is important throughout the process. Parental support is important in the later stages, since many support activities increase as the student becomes more engaged in the college selection process.

SUMMARY AND CONCLUSIONS

The findings detailed in this chapter present an interesting developmental view of the college decision-making process, revealing a contrasting pattern of stability and instability in the educational plans of high school sophomores and juniors.

In their sophomore year,

- students' aspirations remain stable or increase;
- students develop a short list of colleges;
- students develop a list of desirable (albeit unsophisticated) college characteristics;
- students' primary information sources are parents, family members, and peers;
- students are not active in information gathering about colleges; and
- cost and financial aid information is not of primary interest to them (although it is to their parents).

In their junior year,

- students' aspirations remain stable or increase;
- students develop a larger list of colleges, but the types of colleges on the list remain stable and similar;

- students expand their list of college characteristics (which produces more uncertainty);
- students' primary information sources expand to teachers, counselors, and college materials;
- students become active in information gathering about colleges;
- cost and financial aid information becomes of primary interest to students; and
- students begin taking the SAT or the ACT in spring semester.

During the search stage of college choice, students' educational aspirations tended to remain steady or to increase during the sophomore and junior years. Many sophomores aspired to earn college degrees, and most of these students maintained these aspirations in their junior year. The students most likely to change their aspirations were those who did not initially plan to continue their education after high school. By the time they were juniors, more than half of all students who were undecided about their postsecondary plans in their freshman and sophomore years decided they wanted to attend college. Some students who planned to work or to enter military service after high school also shifted their aspirations to a college degree. From this perspective, the college decision-making process of high school students appears stable.

However, we also examined, during students' sophomore and junior years, the stability of their consideration sets and of the institutional characteristics they valued. Here, a very different picture emerges. As early as their sophomore year, students could name the schools they were considering attending and could identify their important characteristics. Although one might intuit that, as juniors, these same students would be more certain about the schools they were considering and the characteristics that were important, we found the reverse to be true: most students were less certain about the characteristics important to them and had added and dropped institutions from their consideration sets in ways that suggest they were not at all certain which institutions they were likely to attend or even what they were looking for.

Surprisingly, student characteristics that we assumed would be associated with greater sophistication, and thus greater certainty about the college decision-making process, had the opposite effect from what we anticipated. Scholastic ability, frequent conversations with parents, and high parental education were associated with less stability and specificity in this phase of the decision-making process. The only intuitive relationship evident was the finding that students who were more actively engaged in gathering information about college had more certainty about the college characteristics important to them.

Most sophomores are not ready for detailed information about colleges. They are not actively engaged in gathering information about colleges and are likely to rely on parents and friends as sources of information. Sophomores are also not interested in information about student financial aid. During their junior year, however, students who plan to attend college become interested in virtually every issue associated with their decision and are actively involved in gathering information. They also consider a larger number of institutions than in their sophomore year. Juniors begin to reach out beyond parents for information about colleges, consulting teachers and counselors. Interestingly, as they gather more information, they become less certain about what they are looking for in a college.

During the search phase, Chapman (1984) postulated that students look for both institutions and institutional attributes. Our findings demonstrate that Chapman is correct. The instability and uncertainty we found during the tenth and eleventh grades are reflective of students who, as they began to more actively search for information, became more confused. As they began to learn more about college, questions arose that increased rather than diminished their uncertainty. Each new piece of information had the potential to raise questions and issues that students had not yet considered. This led to more uncertainty and to the consideration of colleges that students had not seriously thought about before—or indeed had even heard of. Our study suggests that students with good grades, students who talk to their parents and other family members about their educational aspirations, and students with well-educated parents are more confused and uncertain than their peers. We submit, however, that this is a healthy confusion, derived from a wider range of alternatives and a more robust exploration of their options.

Clearly, parents play an important role. Parents who regularly talk to their children about college provide the encouragement necessary to promote a full exploration of educational options. Despite the stereotypes about the relationships between parents and their teenage children, this study suggests that parents have an important effect on this important decision-making process. Our investigation also has implications for such educational initiatives as the Eugene Lang I Have a Dream program and the Twenty-first Century Scholars program funded by the state of Indiana.

From the perspective of high school counselors and college admissions personnel, these results show that guidance and marketing information for sophomores should not be too detailed. They should encourage students to take high school courses and engage in extracurricular activities that keep their educational options open. Parents who have had little formal education may need support to help their students set high educational aspirations and keep their post–high school options open.

PART THREE

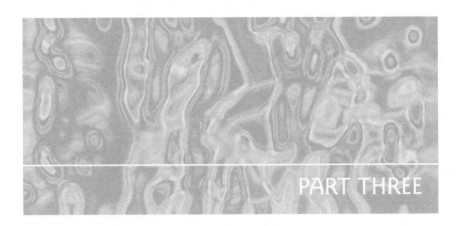

Making Choices

In part 3, we focus on a pivotal year of our study, the senior year in high school. In part 1, we examine the predisposition stage of the college decision-making process of these Indiana high school students, exploring the factors that influenced the development of their aspirations. In part 2, we follow these students as high school sophomores and juniors through the search stage of college choice, our primary focus being those students with postsecondary educational aspirations, looking at the types of college they considered, the characteristic of these colleges that were important to the students, and how actively the students sought information about college options.

Here, we examine the choice stage of the college decision-making process, highlighting the decisions of students in our sample who continued their education after high school graduation. In chapter 5, we continue to track the decisions of the eight students we have been following since the ninth grade. By the time we finished our interviews during their senior year, we had a good idea of their post–high school decisions. In chapter 6, we return to the entire sample for an in-depth look at the factors that influence the postsecondary decisions of high school seniors. Special attention is given to the stability and consistency of students' plans over time and to their knowledge of college costs and financial aid.

5

Following Plans, Changing Plans

In this chapter we follow Allison, Jerome, Laura, Sam, Seth, Michelle, and Todd as they reach closure on their postsecondary plans. By the end of their junior year, three of the eight students appeared to be headed toward work or military service, although one of these students dropped out of our study during her junior year. Todd planned to get a job upon graduation and to hike the Appalachian Trail. Amy, who planned to enter the service after graduation, stopped attending our scheduled interviews halfway through her junior year and did not return our phone calls. Not even her high school counselor was able to help us contact her. Allison ended her junior year with a lack of focus or certainty about her postsecondary plans, but she still appeared more likely to work after high school graduation.

Of the remaining seven students in our interview group, Sam, Seth, and Todd had the most focused plans. Although Jerome, Laura, and Michelle ended their junior year with plans to attend a four-year college, they demonstrated a great deal of uncertainty. Both type of school and, especially for Jerome and Laura, career goals vacillated during their sophomore and junior years.

We continue to trace the consistency of students' plans and aspirations over time and to understand the factors that influenced these plans and aspirations. In addition, we assess the impact of college marketing activities and other sources of information upon these students' college matriculation decisions, to understand the factors that influenced their choices. We also trace the postsecondary decisions of Todd and Allison; the contrast they provide is important.

In chapter 6, we report the results of the analysis of the survey data. The results reveal that parental support and student information gathering are associated with college aspirations. Allison's story, in particular, demonstrates how a student's failure to gather information along with a lack of parental encouragement negatively influences postsecondary decisions.

Our senior-year interviews with Allison continued to reveal a high level of uncertainty and contradiction in her plans and aspirations. During our fall interview, Allison was still thinking about becoming an auto mechanic, even though her mother was opposed to the idea. She also said that she had been considering going to Valparaiso University or the University of Indianapolis but that she had not sent for information because she had decided that the schools were too large. Allison's mother told us that she had encouraged Allison to enter military service but that Allison had showed little interest.

By December, Allison was no longer interested in auto mechanics but was interested in becoming a detective. We asked her what she would have to do to become a detective, but she did not know.

In March, Allison was very uncertain about her career plans, although she told us she had been talking to admissions representatives from Lincoln Tech, a proprietary technical school located in Fort Wayne. She had made several appointments for the representative to come to her house, but each time had canceled the appointment. Allison had also looked into attending Ivy Tech State College, but had subsequently decided against it.

Throughout Allison's senior year, her career and educational goals continued to be contradictory, wandering, and confusing. On more than one occasion, we attempted to probe more deeply and see if she was aware of how contradictory and implausible some of her statements were, but we did not succeed beyond the results already reported. In March, Allison's mother told us that Allison did not know what she wanted to do after graduation but that she herself hoped that Allison would go to a vocational school or college some day. Allison told us she had applied for a clerk's job at K-Mart, but we know from subsequent interviews that she did not get a job at this store.

We do not know whether Allison withheld information from us or whether the contradictions were inherent in her plans. Allison's responses to our questions were limited to yes, no, or I don't know. Her mother also expressed concern about Allison's lack of direction and focus, so our assessment of the evolution of her plans (or lack thereof) is not off the mark.

By her senior year, Allison said that Lincoln was the only school sending her admissions marketing information. She read the information, but she never applied to Lincoln or kept any of the appointments that the admissions staff from Lincoln tried to arrange. She did fill out a financial aid application from Lincoln just before school started in her senior year, but she did not follow up on this. In the December interview, Allison told us that her sisters influenced her thinking about what kind of job to look for after graduating from high school and that her parents, teachers, and high school counselors had not.

Allison indicated that she had not had any conversations with anyone about college costs or about who would pay for college if she matriculated. She said she did not know anything about college loans. Her mother, however, told us that she had told Allison that they would help her pay for a vocational or college education if she wanted to continue her education after high school.

Throughout her senior year, Allison remained the most complex student in our interview group. She seemed unable to formulate any future plan. She was not motivated to gather information about jobs or postsecondary education. As noted in an earlier chapter, Allison did not seem to know "how to get there from here," and every option seemed "too far."

Jerome

During his first senior-year interview, Jerome told us he was definitely going to attend a four-year college. He was still undecided about his major, but unlike the previous year, this uncertainty was no longer causing him to consider not continuing his education immediately after high school graduation.

Jerome's uncertainty about his major persisted throughout the year. In the first three of the four interviews, he said he was undecided about his major. Interestingly, during his last interview, in June, he said he had visited Northwestern University and had decided he wanted to become a mechanical engineer. We noted this shift in plans during our interview with his mother. She replied with a parental form of sarcasm that was simultaneously loving and biting: "Well, later we visited Vincennes University [the only public two-year college in Indiana], and he decided he wanted to major in public relations." We did not interpret either of these statements as a final clarification of Jerome's career plans. Instead, we thought they were further indications of the uncertainty of his academic interests and career goals. Jerome's mother viewed all of these new aspirations as an indication that he was not ready for the demands of college.

In October, Jerome told us that he had requested information from General Motors Institute; he was not sure why, since he was not, at that time, planning to be an engineer. Jerome's primary goal for his collegiate career at that time was to play soccer. This goal, however, did not match his college aspirations. Both Jerome and his mother mentioned that he lacked sufficient size and skill to play soccer at a major university and would have his best chance of playing at a small, private college. Nevertheless, of the schools he was considering in October, Indiana University was his first choice, followed by Purdue University, Ball State University, and Indiana State University, none of which is a small private college. We asked him the number of schools he thought he would submit applications to. He responded, "My brother applied to six or seven schools and was accepted at four. I want to have choices, too."

Jerome was receiving marketing information from the universities listed above and also Ashland College, Illinois Institute of Technology, Kentucky Wesleyan, and Cumberland College. Ashland, Kentucky Wesleyan, and Cumberland were the types of small college at which he might have been able to play soccer, but as we reported in earlier chapters, Jerome's parents sent him clear and consistent messages that they wanted him to go to a public in-state university. In December, Jerome felt he had a chance to get a soccer scholarship from Clemson University in South Carolina. He told us that if this did not work out he would attend Indiana University or Ball State. By March, he had applied to both Ball State and Indiana; he had been admitted to Ball State and was waiting to hear from Indiana. We asked Jerome about his preferences: "If I get into IU, this is where I will go. That's where my brother goes." Jerome also told us that he was still looking into Ashland College, because they, too, might have a scholarship for him.

In June, we conducted our last senior-year interview with Jerome and learned that his scholarship possibilities at Clemson and Ashland had not worked out. We were surprised when Jerome told us he was not going to Indiana University or Ball State but was going to enroll at Vincennes University because that was where his mother wanted him to go. His mother later told us, "I looked at his grades [mostly B's, C's, and D's] and told him that he was not ready for a big place like Indiana or Ball State. I told him he needed to go to a smaller place where he could grow up a little."

We had a strong impression that Jerome's mother and father had made the final decision about where he would enroll. His mother had consistently expressed concern about Jerome's academic performance, though not about his ability. Indeed, at the same time that his mother told us that Jerome was going to Vincennes because of his grades, she also told us that he had done well on his Scholastic Achievement Test (SAT): about 600 on the math section and 400 on the verbal section.

It was obvious in the first interview of the year that Jerome was actively seeking information about college. He was working that year in the guidance office at his high school, and while at work looked up the names of schools with soccer programs and scholarships. Jerome scanned the information mailed from colleges to determine whether the school had academic programs he was interested in or a soccer program. At the end of the year, Jerome told us he did not think that such information had much impact on the schools he seriously considered. However, his mother said she thought Vincennes University had sent out the best information, "and this influenced me—this carried a lot of weight."

In October, Jerome told us he did not expect to pay any of his college costs. He expected his parents to pay and expected to get some financial aid. We asked him if he would be willing to take out loans for college expenses, and he answered that his brother and sister had taken loans, "so I would be willing to take them, too." We are not sure of the accuracy of this statement; later the same day his mother responded to the same question, "No, we definitely do not want him to take out loans." We asked Jerome if his choice of college could be influenced by financial aid, and he indicated that it would. In response to a similar question, his mother told us, "If he gets a soccer scholarship, he can go anywhere—as long it is not too far from home."

Jerome understood federal financial aid programs and institutional athletic scholarships, but he had no understanding of state financial aid programs or academic merit and need-based institutional aid programs. Although Jerome told us that financial aid offers could influence his choice of college, there is little indication that financial aid or total cost played a direct role in his matriculation decision. This may be deceiving, however. In one of our early interviews, Jerome's mother said he should attend a public state school. In his first three years of high school, his parents, especially his mother, played an important role in shaping his plans. In his senior year it appears that his parents set the parameters on the types of school Jerome was seriously considering.

Jerome remained uncertain about his academic and career goals throughout his high school years. Even his choice of which college to attend continued to be uncertain. Our interviews reveal that he learned about colleges from his parents, his siblings, written material in the guidance counselors' office, and material he was mailed. However, Jerome's focus was narrow throughout most of his senior year. The single most important college criteria was whether it had a soccer program and the possibility of his getting an athletic scholarship.

Laura

By October of her senior year, Laura had shifted her career plans again and now wanted to earn a professional degree. Although she was considering fashion merchandising, she was unsure what fashion merchandisers did: "I have talked to my counselor about fashion merchandising. I was looking at whatever those catalogs are. At Eastern Kentucky and at Moorehead State [also in Kentucky], that major is real big. She [my counselor] was talking to me about it. I have talked about it before, but I really don't know what it is. She was just telling me it was something she could see me doing."

At this point, Laura's parents were encouraging her to attend a college or university near home and to live at home. Laura was not enthusiastic: "I don't think I could stand it. You would not have your freedom. . . . At least I wouldn't. Like, at home, you depend on your parents and you still have all these rules and everything." Although Laura mentioned Eastern Kentucky and Moorehead State University, later in the interview she told us she wanted to attend the University of Southern Indiana (USI) because it did not have dormitories. Laura thought that USI was far enough away from home to satisfy her and that "it would be neat" to live in her own apartment. It was not surprising that Laura's parents did not think she was ready to live in an apartment by herself.

By the December interview, Laura was also considering Ball State University, and Laura's mother indicated that she and Laura might visit Eastern Kentucky University (we subsequently learned that they never did). During her junior year, Laura's parents had encouraged her to write to USI, and by now she had applied to and had been admitted to both USI and Ball State. Laura now thought she might major in general studies.

In March, Laura announced that she would attend Ball State instead of USI and live on campus, despite her parents' wishes for her to live at home and commute to USI. She assured us that she was certain of her choice but that her parents still wanted her to live at home and attend either USI or the University of Evansville. In addition, Laura was no longer certain of her course of study: she now planned to major in either law enforcement or radiology.

By her May interview, her plans had changed again. She no longer planned to earn a four-year college degree but rather a two-year degree in radiology. But even this was tentative. She believed she would graduate from USI, but she had heard that the radiology program was very difficult. As a result, she thought there was a good possibility that she would transfer to another degree program.

By October of her senior year, it appeared that Laura had been writing to request information from colleges. She also noted that she was registered to take the SAT. She told us that she had read the information she was sent, but not carefully. The recruitment material she had received had made her think seriously about on-campus housing, admissions entrance requirements, and the sports and social programs offered. We asked her how many colleges she had applied to. In answering this question, Laura gave evidence of not being as proactive in applying to colleges and seeking information as we once thought she was. Her father had written to colleges for her and had applied to USI, Hanover College, and perhaps Ball State for her. "I don't remember. He is the one who got them and filled part of the applications out. So he has done most of it." Laura said that her information came from publications, teachers and counselors, admissions representatives, and college guidebooks but that this information had not had much influence. She did, however, feel that she was well informed about colleges and that she was able to make a good choice.

In October, Laura did not know how much of her college costs her parents would pay. When we asked if she would take out loans to help pay her costs, she responded, "I guess so," but she seemed not to have given it much thought. When we asked if a good financial aid offer might affect her college selection, she said yes.

During our December interview, Laura's mother told us that they would pay all of her college costs, and in an early interview Laura's father had told us that they would not apply for financial aid; experiences with their older daughter had convinced him that they would not receive financial aid. Nevertheless, in December, Laura reported that she had applied for financial aid. Laura was not knowledgeable about student financial aid issues. She understood federal loan programs but knew nothing about federal grants or state financial aid programs. She could not explain how campus-based financial aid programs worked, but she knew that her sister had gotten a scholarship from the private college she attended.

Throughout most of her high school years, Laura revealed great uncertainty about her goals. During her junior and senior years, she vacillated between proprietary schools and public four-year universities and between programs that would require less than two years of study, a two-year degree, and a four-year degree. One of the most striking elements in Laura's educational decision-making process was the involvement of her father. In key areas like investigating colleges and completing college applications, her father did most of the work. And in several instances, her parents ruled out institutions or programs of study that Laura was interested in.

Information about colleges had little effect on Laura's plans or aspirations. Her interest in fashion merchandising is an example of her passive approach to information and information gathering. Although she expressed an interest in fashion merchandising, Laura made no efforts to learn more about the field. Overall, her approach to postsecondary decision making was unfocused and passive.

Sam

Sam entered his senior year with the same motivation and direction that he had in the early years of our study. During our first interview, he informed us that he had received applications from Massachusetts Institute of Technology, General Motors Institute, Rose-Hulman Institute of Technology, Eckerd College, and Wabash College. (He had dropped Purdue from his list because he wanted to go to a small school.) He planned to apply to these schools in November or early December at the latest. He wondered if he could get into MIT and if he would go if he was accepted: "I thought I would give it a shot." Sam, more than any of the other students we interviewed, was clearly getting ready for the transition to college. He even planned to take the SAT for the third time, to see if he could improve his scores.

We were surprised to learn that Sam was considering Eckerd and Wabash, neither of which had an engineering program. But he told us that both had relationships with other universities, where he could earn his engineering degree. In addition, Eckerd had a competitive water-skiing program "that sounds really great; I have always been interested in water skiing." When we asked Sam how much water skiing he had done up to this point, he replied "not much."

When we interviewed Sam in January, he had applied to GMI, Eckerd, Rose-Hulman, Wabash, and Purdue (to the latter "on the spur of the moment"). Of those schools, he had already been admitted to Rose-Hulman and Eckerd. He had gathered all of the financial aid application material from these schools and planned to complete them in February.

At our March interview, Sam had narrowed his choices to Wabash and Eckerd. He liked their liberal arts focus, even though he planned to become an engineer. He was still interested in Rose-Hulman, too, but based upon informal conversations with admissions staff there, Sam was pretty sure he would get larger financial aid offers from Eckerd and Wabash.

By May, Sam had made his college choice: he was going to Eckerd. Both Wabash and Eckerd offered him larger financial aid packages than Rose-Hulman. Eckerd's offer was the largest, but since tuition was also higher at Eckerd, the net cost of attending Wabash was approximately the same as Eckerd. It was clear to us that Sam was enamored with the idea of attending a college in Florida. Once again, he mentioned the water-skiing team. Sam's grandparents lived near the campus, and during a visit to his grandparents over Christmas vacation, Sam had made a trip to the campus. We subsequently learned from his parents that having family members near the college made it easier for them to support Sam's decision. We remembered one of our early interviews with Sam, in which he said that he wanted to attend college near home so he could live with his family. Perhaps the nearness of his grandparents was an important part of his decision.

Sam's parents were supportive of him throughout the process. "My parents would like to influence me, but they are letting me decide." In his senior year, his parents continued to set no limits on the college options Sam was considering. When Sam made his decision, his parents told him they would give him the family's second car and pay for automobile insurance. Although Sam's goals remained focused, he also demonstrated instability in his college planning. The list of colleges he considered changed until well into his senior year. Purdue University was on, off, and back on his consideration set. Compared to the deliberate logic he used in previous years as he explored the various colleges he might attend, his decision to attend Eckerd seemed almost whimsical. Sam had his own reasons to be sure, but they do not appear to be wise to objective observers. We were certainly surprised by his decision but speculated that one consistent part of his plans may have been the desire to be close to family members.

In the fall, Sam estimated that he was receiving fifteen mailings a week from various colleges. Throughout all of our interviews, Sam told us that the admissions marketing information was not influencing his decisions. Nevertheless, he first heard about Eckerd and GMI from unsolicited mail he received. Sam mentioned that his high school principal, in addition to his parents, had told him about several schools and about scholarships.

In the fall, Sam had not thought much about how he would pay for college, but he was knowledgeable about all federal, state, and institutional forms of financial aid. In keeping with Sam's strong goal orientation, he had saved $3,000 toward the cost of his education. He also had no reservations about taking out loans. Borrowing for his education would be the "best investment I ever made." In addition to the scholarship Sam got from Eckerd, he also received through his high school several one-year scholarship awards from local companies. Interestingly, Sam was more concerned about money for college than his parents were. His financial aid award influenced Sam's choice of college, even though his parents consistently told him that they did not want financial aid and total costs to be a significant part of his college-choice decision.

In many ways, Sam presents a sharp contrast to the other students. During his senior year, he had clear educational goals and was actively pursuing them. More than any other student in our interview sample, Sam exemplified the college search activities associated with college-bound students who are considering a clear set of colleges and who move through the process in a relatively linear and systematic fashion. Even Sam, however, revealed instability in his consideration set. His list of potential colleges ranged from a large public university with an engineering program (Purdue) to out-of-state schools (like MIT). His list also included two small liberal arts colleges without engineering programs. He finally selected a liberal arts college because of the scholarship they offered and because they had a water-skiing team. Thus, even for focused students like Sam, the final selection of a college is not entirely linear, logical, and predictable.

Seth

Over the first four years of our study, Seth's plan evolved from a plan to go to work immediately after high school to earning a four-year college degree. In his junior year, he planned to earn a two-year vocational degree. In October of his senior year, he planned to go to Vincennes University for two years then transfer to Purdue University to major in wildlife management.

We asked Seth about the reasons for the changes in his aspirations: "For one thing, I had a job this summer working around cars, and I discovered I get headaches around gasoline. I started to think about this more seriously, about having a career. You are going to need college. I like the outdoors and enjoy being out in the woods and stuff. I talked to someone who was going to Purdue for wildlife management." He next contacted Purdue: "They told me stuff about the number of job placements and that kind of stuff. Right now, for the people in wildlife management, there is a need to go into the field. There is a lack of people there."

In the October interview with his mother, she said, "He finally knows what he wants to do. I kept telling him there was no big hurry. He just came to me one day and said that he knew what he wanted to do." By December, Seth had been admitted to Vincennes. His plans never wavered, he never applied to any other school, and he enrolled in Vincennes the following fall. Seth credited his parents with constant support and encouragement. They reminded him when college representatives were visiting his high school, took him to financial aid information programs, and took him on college visits. They also assured him that they would provide all the financial assistance necessary and that they expected him to repay them once he earned his degree and had a job.

Seth had actively gathered information from his high school guidance office and colleges. However, he did not make any campus visits until after he had already decided to attend Vincennes. He applied to Vincennes in October and was accepted in December. Seth told us that college admissions material, admissions representatives, college guidebooks, college fairs, friends, parents, and publications he received from the Indiana Career and Postsecondary Advancement Center (ICPAC) were all helpful in his decision making. He rated college alumni and currently enrolled students as very helpful and teachers and high school counselors as not helpful. Interestingly, when we asked him if this information had influenced his decision, he said no. But his mother confided that the information Seth had received from ICPAC and his participation in our research project (which had an indirect affiliation with the organization) had enhanced Seth's educational aspirations. She had contacted Purdue directly to ask about wildlife management and their perceptions of the program at Vincennes and told us that Purdue had been helpful and that the information had at least influenced her, if not Seth.

In the second semester of his senior year, Seth could give general definitions of federal grants, loans, and work-study programs. He was not well informed about state scholarship programs. He had some information about the institutional scholarship programs at Vincennes and planned to apply for one or more of them. Seth told us that he expected his parents to pay about 50 percent of his college costs and that he would pay the rest. Seth's mother told us that he already had a certificate of deposit saved in a bank. Since Seth focused upon one school so early in his senior year, questions of cost, or how aid might influence him to attend another school, were not relevant. Generally, it is our sense that financial concerns were not a major factor in Seth's decision.

Michelle

In October of her senior year, Michelle still planned to earn a bachelor's degree from a four-year college, but her plans, like Laura's, were inconsistent. Michelle was considering two church-related colleges, Andrews University (in Michigan) and Oakwood College (in Alabama), and two historically black colleges, Morehouse College (in Atlanta) and Howard University (in Washington, D.C.). It did not appear that she had done anything to learn about Morehouse or Howard.

Then, Michelle informed us that she was going to enroll in Indiana Business College (IBC), a proprietary school that does not award four-year degrees. IBC, she said, was close to home and, in addition, she could earn a degree there in only fourteen months and then get a good job. By December, Michelle had been admitted to IBC. Her mother said, "I like the idea of Michelle going to IBC because they offer courses specifically related to getting a job, and they would permit her to take refresher courses if she needs them," adding that Michelle could "always finish her four-year degree if she wants to."

By March, Michelle had changed plans once again, telling us she was going to Andrews. Her reasons for this selection were that Andrews was operated by the church she belonged to, she knew people who went to Andrews, and it was not far from home. Her mother supported this plan because Andrews was affiliated with her church and close to home. However, when we asked Michelle's mother if she was certain Michelle would attend Andrews and graduate, her mother replied, "I don't know. We will take it one day at a time." In March, Michelle had not yet applied to Andrews but told us she was preparing to do so.

By May, Michelle's plans had changed, and she now planned to attend Oakwood. She had not yet applied for admission to Oakwood or for financial aid, saying she would take care of both applications in the summer. Michelle's reason for selecting Oakwood was twofold: it was operated by the church she attended, and its student body was mostly African American. This was a surprising turn of events, but the choice did meet her expressed interest in attending a church-related college and a historically black college.

In the fall, Michelle reported that she had been actively gathering information, asking friends, teachers, and counselors for information and advice. She had also written to request information and had made campus visits to IBC and Andrews. She had not yet taken the SAT and, in fact, never did take the SAT. By December, Michelle reported that she had received, at the rate of two or three a week, mailings from two or three dozen proprietary schools, colleges, and universities. She said the mailings had influenced her college choices but could not say just how.

Michelle indicated that she was aware of and understood federal grant and loan programs but had never heard of any state or campus-based financial aid programs. Michelle told us that the cost of college was a major concern for her and her mother but that she was willing to pay whatever she had to in order to attend. She would take out loans if necessary, she said, but was concerned about how much money she should borrow, since she was not sure how much she could afford to repay after she finished college.

Michelle's senior year revealed the same pattern of change as Jerome's and Laura's. While her career plans and academic interests remained relatively stable, her college choice shifted considerably over the course of her last year in high school. For most of the students in this study, there is little evidence that the information they received from significant others and from colleges and universities had much influence on their decisions. The other pattern is their lack of information about and awareness of state and institutional financial aid programs. At the end of Michelle's senior year, there was still a great deal of uncertainty in her postsecondary plans. It appeared to us that Michelle might still not know or really understand what the "inside" of a college was like.

Todd

At the start of his senior year, Todd's plans continued to be focused. He planned to sign up for the U.S. Marines some time in the fall semester and arrange a date to report for training that would give him time to hike the Appalachian Trail over the summer. Unlike some students in our study who did not plan to continue their formal education after high school, Todd was earning mostly B's and C's. He noted that he had to do well if he was to qualify for advanced training in the marines. In our fall interview with Todd's mother, she was supportive of his plans and said that Todd talked about his plans frequently with her and her husband and that Todd's older brothers also thought Todd had done a good job of charting his future.

In the spring of his senior year, however, things started to change for Todd. He was concerned that he might not be able to join the marines. He had not passed his first physical because of poor eyesight. The local recruiter for the marines, who had befriended Todd during their many conversations, told Todd to come back and take the eye exam one more time. He also told Todd that he would see if an exception might be made for Todd, telling Todd, "You're just the kind of person we really want and I'll see if I can do something to help you." When we asked Todd what he would do if he were not able to join the marines, he replied, "I'm not sure."

By our spring interview, Todd had been turned down by the marines. Surprisingly, he did not seem despondent. He was not sure what he was going to do over the long term, but he was sure that he would undertake his planned hike of the Appalachian Trail. He had completely mapped out his hike, had been saving to purchase the equipment he needed, and his parents were going to give him a new lightweight backpack as a graduation present. We asked what he would do when he finished the hike; Todd responded that he was a hard worker and was certain he could find a good job locally.

SUMMARY

By the end of the senior year, we had lost contact with one of our eight students. Of the seven remaining students, we found the full range of postsecondary planning. Todd and Sam remained goal oriented and consistently proactive in their efforts to achieve their goals. Jerome, Michelle, and Seth wavered in their planning and decision making but were, nevertheless, actively engaged in planning their future, continuing to explore alternatives and seek information.

Allison and Laura demonstrated lower levels of goal orientation and information seeking, Allison being the most uncertain and least goal oriented. In some ways, even Amy appeared to be more goal oriented than Allison. In all cases but Amy's, the parents in our interview group were supportive and appeared to have good communication with their children. Sam's parents provided clear and unambiguous support for college attendance and for exploring a wide range of four-year colleges. Todd's parents offered similarly high levels of support and encouragement for his plans. Jerome's mother and Laura's father were key figures in shaping the kinds of college these students considered. Indeed, Laura's father may have been too involved in her decision making, an overinvolvement that continued after Laura graduated from high school. Michelle's mother was supportive of her plans but did not provide the same level of direct guidance as Sam's, Jerome's, Laura's, or Seth's parents. In Seth's case, his parents' saving for his college education and his mother's efforts to keep him informed about financial aid and about college representatives' visits to his high school were tangible forms of support and encouragement. Although Allison's parents obviously cared about her and were supportive, their support was less tangible and focused.

In the following three chapters we examine trends from the larger sample of students and see how things turned out for the remaining students.

6

The Complexities of the Senior Year

Our longitudinal study, which began in 1986 with a large sample of ninth-grade students in Indiana, had two focuses: (1) the chronological development of the postsecondary plans and aspirations of high school students and (2) the people and experiences that influence these plans. By the twelfth grade, the students were beginning to complete their plans. Their aspirations were no longer abstract thoughts loosely connected to a distant future. Instead, the future was now upon them.

In chapter 5, some trends are evident among our interview group. For each student except Sam, we saw evidence that even in the senior year students are uncertain about their plans for the future. It might not be surprising that they were still sorting out which college to attend or where they might begin to look for their first job, but the majority of these students were still struggling with the more basic issues of what kind of work they wanted to do and whether they would continue their formal education. For Jerome and Laura, their interests and college plans varied widely throughout the year. Seth's educational aspirations and plans, on the other hand, steadily grew firmer and more ambitious. Although Sam remained focused regarding his educational plans, he too exhibited some surprising shifts in the type of college he was considering, and indeed, his final college decision surprised all of us. For all of the students in our sample except Sam, respondents did not finalize their plans until late in their senior year. Thus, the developmental process that we have been tracking did not culminate in final decisions until the spring of their senior year—and, as we will discover in succeeding chapters, some students changed their minds again after that.

In this chapter, we turn to most of the same themes we considered in chapter 5. Using findings from interview data and from surveys from the larger samples and focusing on the senior year, we examine the following questions:

For those students who aspired to attend college, did the number and types of college they were considering change? When did students finalize their plans? How active were they in gathering information about their career or educational options? To what extent did family members, friends, teachers and counselors, college admissions personnel, and college marketing activities influence their decisions? How much did they know about college costs and student financial aid? How much did concerns about costs and financial aid influence their plans?

CONSISTENCY OF PLANS AND ASPIRATIONS

As students progressed from their freshman year through their senior year, fewer of them were undecided about their plans upon graduation and more of them planned to attend college: by the senior year, only 9 percent were either undecided or did not plan to eventually continue their formal education. This figure undoubtedly overstates the case, because students who did not plan to attend college were less likely to return their surveys. Nevertheless, there was a demonstrable shift by the senior year toward plans to attend college and even to attend graduate school. Nearly 75 percent of respondents reported throughout their high school years that they planned to go to college.

Parental support and encouragement played a key role in the educational aspirations of students between the ninth and eleventh grades, and we continued to look at the role of parents during the twelfth grade. We found an interesting pattern, one so central to our research that we highlight the results in this chapter and the next. We discovered that for some students the educational expectations of their parents began to decline. Although most parents in our sample indicated in the ninth-grade year that they expected their student to attend college, by the twelfth grade some parents had changed their minds, especially parents with low incomes, low educational level, and whose student had a low grade point average. While this shift was not pronounced, the relationship is statistically significant.

This shift in parents' expectations may signal a similar shift in students' expectations. College-bound high school seniors decreased the number of schools in their consideration sets and began to develop more realistic consideration sets (see also Litten, Sullivan, and Brodigan, 1983). This finding may provide insight into why the educational plans and aspirations of some students change over time.

To examine the stability in students' consideration sets, we looked at the number of colleges and the specific colleges students considered in their sophomore year and in their senior year.[1] The average number of schools considered by sophomores was approximately two, rising to more than three in the junior year but falling to three in the senior year. This pattern suggests that in the junior year students more actively explored college options and in the senior year, as they evaluated their options, began to narrow their choices. A large multistate study of the college decision-making process found similar results for high school seniors (see Litten, Sullivan, and Brodigan, 1983; their study, however, did not include high school juniors). From both a public and institutional policy perspective, the findings show that the junior year may be the best time to influence students' college options. When we compared tuition costs and admissions selectivity of the colleges students were considering in the tenth and twelfth grades, we found a high degree of stability. (We used criteria from *Peterson's Guide* and categorical ratings of college tuition costs.) In admissions selectivity of colleges, 87 percent of the students' consideration sets were consistent. In tuition costs, 78 percent were consistent.

Another measure of stability is whether the specific institutions considered by sophomores were still being considered by these students in their senior year. Only about 12 percent of the first choices in the tenth grade were still these students' first choices when they were seniors. However, 59 percent of the tenth-grade first choices remained in the consideration sets in the twelfth grade.

We compared the characteristics and activities of students who had stable plans with students whose plans changed over time. Few students reported decreases in aspirations between the ninth and twelfth grade: nearly 75 percent of ninth graders who planned to continue their formal education after high school still planned to do so as seniors, and in fact the trend was toward increased educational aspirations. So few students reported lowered educational aspirations that we lacked enough respondents to analyze these students, and thus we compared only students whose educational aspirations remained constant (they always aspired to continue their education after high school) with students whose postsecondary plans changed between ninth and twelfth

1. We would have liked to look at changes during the sophomore, junior, and senior years in a continuous, longitudinal fashion; however, for reasons we were unable to determine, there was limited overlap in the students who responded to the tenth-, eleventh-, and twelfth-grade surveys. The idiosyncracies of our response rates each year enabled us to compare the responses of sophomores and juniors, juniors and seniors, or sophomore and seniors, but not sophomore, juniors, and seniors. We focus on the differences in students' consideration sets between the tenth and twelfth grades because they provide the most interesting comparisons.

grades. These changes were predominantly away from being undecided, away from working after high school, away from joining the military service after high school, and toward planning for college. Compared with students whose plans changed, seniors with stable educational plans reported talking about their plans more to their parents than to their peers, teachers, or counselors. Seniors with stable plans also tended to come from families with higher incomes and to have parents with higher levels of education. They also had higher grade point averages and were more likely to have been active in gathering information about colleges. These students were interested even in ninth grade in receiving information about colleges.

When we compared consideration sets, one pattern emerges when the focus is on number of institutions and another pattern is evident when the focus is on admissions selectivity and tuition cost. By the latter measure, students evidenced more stability if they had higher grade point averages; if they reported talking more with peers, teachers, counselors, and alumni than with their parents; and if they were involved in searching for information and institutions. Given the importance of consistent interaction with and support by parents to sustain educational aspirations, these findings are intriguing.

However, if we use a numerical count of institutions in the consideration sets, another relationship is apparent. Compared to seniors whose consideration sets had narrowed, students whose consideration sets had expanded by their senior year were more likely to talk to peers, teachers, counselors, and alumni than to their parents. These students also had higher grade point averages. Seniors who were considering an increasing number of colleges also were looking at more selective and more expensive schools. This shift to greater reliance on sources of information outside of parents and other family members is noteworthy. The shift to external sources of information is evident in many ways throughout the senior year. In fact, an increased use of sources of information external to students' immediate families was so apparent that it caused us to develop conceptual models to identify this shift.

From this conceptual perspective, we suggest that throughout most of the developmental years of schooling the postsecondary aspirations of youth are shaped primarily by parents and, to a lesser extent, by siblings—*internal* sources of influence and information. However, beginning during the junior year and more prominently in the senior year, peers, teachers, counselors, and even college marketing material become more influential sources of information. These *external* sources of information exert a strong impact on the postsecondary educational decisions of students. The fact that seniors with higher educational aspirations and those considering more selective colleges talked more to peers, teachers, and counselors than to their parents surprised us, but we offer the following explanation. By the time students are in the twelfth grade, they have started to formulate clearer ideas about postsecondary education and what they are looking for in a school. Developmentally, they are making the break from relying on their parents to make decisions for them. Although parents have had a major effect on students' consideration sets, as students move closer to making their postsecondary matriculation decision, they seek information and opinions from peers, teachers, and counselors both about college attributes and about specific institutions. Both Jerome and Michelle learned about some of the schools they considered from guidance counselors, peers, and church members.

The patterns of relationships reveal the intricacies of the college decision-making process. Early in our study, the relationships were predictable and uncomplicated. For example, we consistently found that the extent to which students talked to parents and the amount of parental support for postsecondary education, along with academic performance in high school, were the best predictors of college aspirations. However, as we examined the process that students used to identify potential schools to attend, our methods of analysis by necessity became more complex. By the time students reached their junior and senior years, we found it necessary to use student background characteristics and college search activities to explain the types of school students were considering and were even able to understand why some students were narrowing or expanding their consideration sets. However, we could not predict the specific institutions they were considering. Sam, Laura, and Michelle are good examples of how students can ultimately make decisions that seem to be ill advised and even irrational to any objective outsider.

MAKING FINAL PLANS

When do studentss begin to apply to colleges? When do they apply for financial aid? When do they take college admissions tests? Answers to these questions provide insights into when students begin to solidify their college-choice decisions and can help high school counselors and college admissions professionals determine the most useful time for providing these students with information and services.

According to Lewis and Morrison (1975), most high school seniors conduct serious evaluations of the schools they are considering between October and April. Half of them make applications over a seven-week period between early November and early January, another 10 percent apply in October, and the remaining 40 percent by early April. Women apply earlier than men. Stewart et al. (1987), in a retrospective survey of college first-year students at Michigan State University, found that 10 percent decided what college to attend during their junior year, 70 percent during their senior year, and 20 percent after their senior year.

While our study does not permit us to identify the specific months in which students applied to college, it does enable us to identify key time periods. At the time of our October interviews with our subsample of students and parents, 27 percent of the students had applied to at least one college. Our fall survey of high school seniors was completed in November; by that time, only 6 percent had applied to any school (89% planned to apply before the end of the semester). (These findings may be surprising, given the focus of the media on a small number of elite colleges and on the students applying to them. These students often apply very early and to many institutions, and many of them are not accepted at these institutions. News reports regarding this small portion of colleges and their applicants do not, however, accurately portray the situation for the majority of colleges and the students who apply to them. The majority of students who apply to college do not apply early, and the majority of them are admitted.)

Although the majority of the students in our study had not yet applied to schools, they were taking steps to prepare to apply. Fifty-five percent of the interview group had taken at least one of the entrance exams one or more times. Another 10 percent reported planning to take it in the future. In the survey group, 64 percent had taken either the SAT or the ACT by November, and another 16 percent planned to take one of these tests (42% had either taken the SAT or the ACT exam twice, or they planned to). In the jargon of admissions testing, the state of Indiana is "an SAT state," meaning that higher education institutions prefer the SAT for making admissions decisions. By November, Sam had taken the SAT twice, Jerome had taken it once, and Laura, Sam, and Michelle planned to take it some time before the end of the school year.

By the fall interviews, most students had not yet applied for student financial aid. Since the federal government does not usually release the free application for federal student aid (FAFSA) until January, this finding is not surprising. (A small number of students planning to attend private colleges might have completed financial aid forms created by the institutions. This study was conducted before a consortium of private colleges decided to use the College Board's college scholarship service to develop a more detailed financial aid profile of families than the FAFSA provides.) Most of the fifty-six students who planned to attend college had requested financial aid information, even though they saw this area as primarily the responsibility of their parents. And it is true that nearly all financial aid forms require detailed information about family income that students could not complete (unless they applied as an independent student with little or no financial support from their parents).

By March of their senior year, most of the students in our interview sample who were planning to attend college had applied for student financial aid. By April, when the second student survey data were collected, 90 percent of survey respondents were either "informed" or "well informed" about student financial aid. Sam applied for financial aid early in February, with his parents' help. Jerome applied in March, with prodding and assistance from his mother. Laura and Michelle submitted applications in March. In Laura's case, her father submitted the application, though he acknowledged that he did not expect Laura to be eligible for financial aid.

The timing of these activities suggests that students need information about admissions testing as early as their junior year and no later than the fall of their senior year. Students are still actively developing their consideration sets at the start of their senior year, and most of them do not apply until after November, but they do plan to during this first semester. High school semesters typically end in December or January. Therefore, October, November, and December may be the most effective months for high school guidance counselors and college admissions officers to provide assistance to students. Students and their parents start thinking about applying for financial aid in October and November and actually apply during a short period between January and March. Therefore, assistance and detailed information about student financial aid applications, procedures, and programs should be provided between December and March. (To be eligible for state of Indiana grants, Indiana residents must file the FAFSA by March 1.)

CHANGING SOURCES OF INFORMATION

Throughout this longitudinal study, we explored the influence of family members, peers, teachers, counselors, and college marketing activities on the college decision-making process. A corollary question is how active were students in gathering information about educational opportunities?

Students who throughout their high school years sustained their plans to attend college had high grade point averages and parents with high levels of education and income. However, of most statistical significance was that these students had frequent conversations with their parents about their plans and had their parents' support for their plans. This suggests that internal sources of support and information are important for the early development and the persistance of students' educational goals. These internal sources of support and information may lead to increased confidence among students in their educational goals. Educators and community resource people can influence educational aspirations and plans indirectly by assisting and educating parents about the important role they play in the lives of their children.

Our research also indicates that external sources of information—peers, counselors, teachers, alumni, and colleges— influence the choice stage of college decision making. Sam, for example, learned of some of the schools he considered during his junior and senior year from his high school principal. Michelle learned about the church-related colleges and the historically black colleges she considered from friends and people at her church. Jerome looked into DePauw University on the recommendation of his high school counselor. Considering a wide range of educational options is worthwhile for students. Jackson (1982) observed that many students fail to find colleges that are a good match with their abilies and interests because they consider a too-narrow range of institutions and posited that this may be the reason many college students drop out.

The surveys from the twelfth grade reveal more information-gathering activities on the part of all students planning to attend college. Compared with the junior year, students were more likely to request information from schools, to make campus visits, to talk to admissions representatives, and to seek out college alumni. (Never during our interviews or in our surveys did students attach much importance to the influence of college admissions counselors. However, in later chapters our research presents a different perspective on the role of admissions professionals.) In addition, students planning to attend the more selective schools more actively gathered information than students planning to attend public colleges and less selective colleges. We asked students who were not planning to continue their education whether they had sought information about careers or jobs and also whether they had taken career aptitude tests. Consistently, these students engaged in less information gathering than students who intended to go on to college.

By placing students along a continuum, with those who did not plan to continue their education as having the lowest educational aspirations and those who planned to attend more selective institutions as having the highest educational aspirations, a pattern emerges.[2] Students who earn higher grades may be more likely to be singled out by teachers, counselors, and colleges. They are offered suggestions about their future and are sent information. This information—and their academic success— may lead them to ask questions and also to gain confidence in their futures. This pattern may repeat itself over and over again during the high school years.

During the four interviews conducted in the senior year with the subsample of students, students did not attribute much direct influence on their

2. We include in "selective institutions" private colleges, because their patterns in our analyses are similar.

choice of college to college marketing materials. In earlier work, Chapman (1981) found that most printed admissions material had little impact on matriculation decisions and concluded that students used these materials only for confirming information. The responses of students in our interview group provides mixed support for this assertion. Sam first learned about Eckerd College from mail he received from the college. He did not decide to attend Eckerd because of these mailings, but he did first learn about the school from them. Seth and his mother told us that his participation in the Indiana Career and Postsecondary Advancement Center program, and all of the information he received because of this participation, had an important influence on his decisions. For Allison, Jerome, Michelle, and Laura, college marketing information appears to have had little impact.

These mixed findings are also true of our surveys. In November of their senior year, nearly 14 percent of the students reported that the information they had received in the mail from colleges had a great influence, another 46 percent said it had some influence, about 40 percent said it had almost no influence. If we combine the categories of "great" influence and "some" influence, then 60 percent of the respondents stated that information they received in the mail had at least some influence. If we group "some" and "little" influence, we can conclude that 86 percent of all students reported that admissions marketing information had at best only some influence. If we use a definition of information that includes not only mailed information but conversations with peers, teachers, counselors, and college alumni, there is evidence to support the importance of these sources of information.[3]

UNDERSTANDING COLLEGE COSTS AND FINANCIAL AID

Perhaps no other topic related to postsecondary education has attracted more public attention than student financial aid and college costs. Newspaper and magazine articles on student financial aid programs and rising college costs

3. Much of the previous research conducted on the influence of these external sources of information concluded that they exerted little or no influence on the college-choice process (Hossler, Braxton, and Coopersmith, 1989). Most of these studies, however, were flawed because they asked students after they had chosen a college and often after they were already enrolled . The longitudinal nature of this study overcomes these weaknesses and indicates that the role of external sources of information depends upon the stage of the college decision-making process being studied. They have little influence on students' aspirations but appear to have some influence on their consideration sets.

appear regularly. Both the public and elected officials are concerned about the affordability of college. Given the importance of these issues, our study focused on the following questions: Were high school seniors and their parents knowledgeable about college costs? Were they knowledgeable about federal and state financial aid programs? And what was the impact of costs and student financial aid upon the decision to attend college. We explored these issues in the surveys administered in April of the students' senior year and in the November survey sent to parents. The questions included the following concerns:

- How informed did both students and parents judge themselves to be about college financial aid programs and their eligibility for student financial aid?
- How certain were students and parents that they would be able to pay for college?
- How would financial aid awards affect matriculation decisions?

Students (70%) and parents (87%) indicated that they were either "well informed" or "informed" about financial aid programs and about their eligibility for financial aid. Given the consistent pattern evident in our study that students perceive their parents to be responsible for college costs and financial aid, it is not surprising that students were not as informed as their parents.

Parents have relatively low levels of knowledge about specific financial aid programs—56 percent were "informed" or "well informed" about state grant programs and federal loan programs; and 52 percent were "informed" or "well informed" about state scholarship programs. These lower levels of knowledge suggest that parents are not as knowledgeable about financial aid when asked a less global question. However, these answers may reflect differences in information because of a program's relevance for the family. If parents do not think the family will be eligible for a federal Pell grant, they are not likely to spend time learning the details of this grant. Despite these seeming contradictions, we were impressed with the level of knowledge displayed in our interview group during the junior year and the response of parents to the global question about their knowledge of student financial aid.

Regarding certainty about their ability to pay for college, seniors (70%) and parents (63%) reported similar levels. We followed up this question by asking how much of the total costs students thought their parents were likely to pay. Nearly 20 percent expected that their parents would pay all of their college costs, 30 percent expected they would pay three-fourths of the costs, 20 percent expected they would pay half of the costs, 17 percent expected they would pay one-fourth of the costs, and 13 percent did not expect their parents to pay any of the costs. Interestingly, the more students expected their parents to pay, the more certain both students and parents were that they would be able to pay for college. We hypothesize that the amount students expect their parents to pay is correlated with the amount of support and sacrifice parents are willing to make. Parents who are willing to pay more are more certain they can pay because they have already decided to make whatever sacrifices are necessary to ensure that their children go to college. In addition, and perhaps most important, these parents have communicated these attitudes to their children.

Finally, we examined the effects of financial aid in matriculation decisions. This analysis is most useful for college administrators who try to induce students to enroll at their institutions. Federal and state financial aid is intended to promote access to college; it is not intended to promote the decision to attend one school over another. The use of campus financial aid to recruit students is not widely used at proprietary vocational schools. It is common practice, however, at private colleges and is becoming increasingly common at public schools.

How much are students' matriculation decisions influenced by campus-based financial aid? When doing this kind of analysis, it is difficult to determine whether we are looking at the economic effects of financial aid or the psychic effects of financial aid. Financial aid lowers the net cost of attendance for students and parents, so the positive effects of financial aid may be strictly a lower net cost of attendance (the economic effect). But Jackson (1978), Freeman (1984), and Abrahamson and Hossler (1990) have observed that receiving aid is often more important than the amount of financial aid, because aid becomes a substantive way for institutions to communicate that "we want you to be part of our community" (the psychic effects). Given the range of issues explored in our longitudinal study, it was not possible to include a sufficient number of questions for us to untangle the economic and psychic benefits of financial aid offers. In addition, our study measured only the perceived or probable effect of financial aid, not the actual effect. Most of the students in their senior year still did not know if they would receive financial aid or how much they would receive.

Parents were asked to estimate the influence of various amounts of financial aid on the advice they would offer to their children as to which institution to attend. Their responses suggest that relatively small amounts of financial aid ($500 to $1,000) would exert only modest influence on their advice to students but that moderate-sized awards ($1,001 to $3,000) would have a strong influence (see figure 6.1).

We also asked students whether a financial aid offer from a school would influence their matriculation decision; 51 percent said it would have "some" effect or a "strong" effect, and 49 percent said it would have a "small" effect or "no" effect. Since no amount was specified, we cannot be precise about the

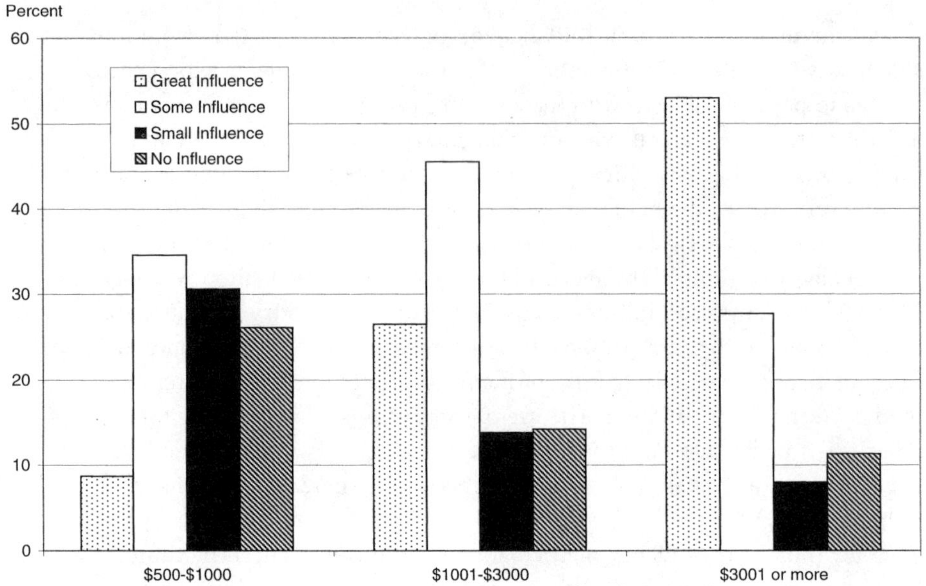

FIGURE 6.1 Influence of Financial Aid on Parental Advice

amount of money it would take to influence students' enrollment decisions. Parents' responses suggest that it would take only relatively small amounts, but during most of our interviews, most parents and students indicated that financial aid alone would not have much impact on matriculation decisions. Many parents and students in the subsample said that attending an in-state public college that was close to home was more important than financial aid awards. Jerome looked for schools offering soccer scholarships but, more important, for schools where he could play soccer. Michelle (as reported in a later chapter) dropped out of college after her first year because she did not get enough financial aid. Sam rejected a smaller scholarship from Wabash College to go to Eckerd, even though in reality the net cost of attendance was higher at Eckerd.

The most definitive research on the effects financial aid examined the effects of aid awards on the matriculation decisions of high-ability high school seniors (Chapman and Jackson, 1987). These researchers concluded that it would take at least $2,000 to moderately increase the probability that a student would enroll in their second-choice instead of their first-choice college. To increase the probability by 50 percent required aid awards of more than $5,000. The Chapman and Jackson sample included only high-ability students, many of whom were considering private colleges. Students in our Indiana study had a wider range of student ability, and most of them planned to attend public colleges. The survey data raises the possibility that for students with lower grade point averages who are considering attending lower-cost, in-state, public universities, fewer institutional financial aid dollars might be required to influence their enrollment decisions.

SUMMARY

The findings reported in this study demonstrate that an intricate web of factors influences the choice stage of college decision making. Parents, peers, teachers, counselors, and college-marketing activities interact with student grade point averages, perceptions of college costs and financial aid, and students' information-gathering activities to influence the stability of their educational plans and the number and types of colleges they consider.

The following are the developmental characteristics of the decision-making process of high school seniors:

- Their aspirations remain stable or increase.
- Their educational expectations differ from their parents.
- Students who have not yet taken the SAT or the ACT are likely take it in the fall semester.
- Students' information gathering reaches its peak.
- Students' peers, teachers, and counselors replace parents, family, and peers as information sources.
- Both students and parents are more knowledgeable about costs and financial aid.
- The number of colleges on students' consideration sets decreases, but the types of college remain the same.
- Most students apply to college between October and January.
- Most parents complete the financial aid applications between January and March.

The support, encouragement, and information that families and high schools provide affect whether students plan to continue their education after high school and what kinds of school they consider. Ongoing support and encouragement from parents is especially critical. (The discovery that some parents' educational expectations for their children declined is an interesting result and is examined in the next chapter.) Students whose parents encourage their college plans throughout high school and students with high grade point averages are likely to have stable educational aspirations. In addition, their consideration sets are more stable as measured by college selectivity and cost.

The findings also reveal an interesting pattern in the influence of resources outside of parents and the family over time. Teachers, counselors, and other external sources of information do not exert a strong influence on the postsecondary educational aspirations of freshmen and sophomores. However, by the time these students are juniors and seniors, these external sources do have an effect. Older students who talk more to peers, teachers, and counselors have more stable educational aspirations, and the selectivity and the tuition costs of the schools they consider are also more stable. These students more actively engage in requesting information, reading college guides, and making campus visits. Students who talk more with peers, teachers, and counselors and who more actively engage in information-gathering activities also consider a larger number of schools. If Jackson (1982) is correct, an increase in sources of external information may lead to a consideration of a wider array of educational institutions, to greater satisfaction with school choice, and to a greater likelihood that students will finish their degree program.

In the following chapter, we examine what the students in our study actually did after graduating from high school. These findings, which support Jackson's, have policy implications for high school teachers and guidance counselors, whose role in the choice decision is obviously important. Guidance can be given in informal one-on-one mentoring sessions, but it should also be available in organized group guidance sessions, which provide more efficient outreach. These professionals need preservice or in-service preparation for this important role; few education or counseling programs equip these educators for such functions. Students with lower grade point averages and with less parental support are not as likely to seek out the support and information they need to help them achieve their goals. We should consider intrusive school and community advising programs to enable these students to sustain their college plans. For some students, opportunities for apprenticeships and on-the-job training may help them learn about possible careers and in making postsecondary plans.

The analyses also show that college direct marketing and recruitment activities had an effect on the choice stage, although its extent was difficult to measure. If we combine two student responses, approximately 60 percent of respondents reported that institutional marketing activities had at least "some" influence on the schools they considered. However, we could combine responses differently and conclude that for 86 percent college marketing activities had at least a "little" influence on their decisions. Although many educators and parents are critical of college marketing efforts, these efforts may help shape and sustain students' educational plans. In addition, family-, school-, and community-based efforts to organize and provide transportation for visits to colleges can help students expand their consideration sets and learn more about the institutions they are considering. To be most useful, these activities need to culminate in the early fall of the senior year, since most students decide on the schools to apply to in late fall through early winter.

Our results provide insights into how much influence financial aid awards have on enrollment decisions. By the senior year, almost 90 percent of students and parents believed they were informed about federal financial aid programs and their eligibility, a significant increase in number of parents and an even more dramatic increase in number of students knowledgeable about student financial aid. Both students and parents expected parents to play the primary role in paying for college and in taking care of financial aid: almost 50 percent of students anticipated that their parents would pay between 75 percent and 100 percent of their college expenses; more than 63 percent of parents and 70 percent of students were certain that parents would be able to pay the student's college expenses. Indeed, the more parents expected to pay, the more certain they were that they could afford to pay. We speculate that these parents had been committed to their children's postsecondary education for years, that they had saved toward college expenses, that their incomes were high, and that they were willing to make sacrifices for their children's education.

The process of applying for financial aid and managing the costs of college are especially important to parents. Efforts by federal agencies, state agencies, colleges, and local high schools to inform parents on these matters are important in enabling parents to assist their children to achieve their educational goals. Often, efforts to provide information and coach families about student financial aid are targeted at students. Although this may be an effective way to reach out to families, policy makers and educators should not forget that in most instances the parents are the primary audience for financial aid and college cost information.

In part 4, we look at what students did after they finished high school. The first interviews were conducted in January, eight months after the students graduated from high school. The second was conducted during the summer four years after they had graduated.

PART FOUR

Dreams Realized, Unrealized, or Deferred

This study, unlike many earlier studies, followed students after graduation from high school, and the knowledge of what happened after high school makes the research presented in this book unique. The breadth of information gathered adds a significant dimension to the student college-choice research base.

We surveyed the large sample of students for the last time in January 1991. During the summer of that same year, we conducted telephone interviews with our subsample. These final surveys and interviews enabled us to search for additional relationships between the postsecondary plans of these high school students and their subsequent decisions. These results are discussed in chapter 7.

During the summer after the 1993-94 academic year, we conducted the final telephone interviews with the fifty-six families in our sample. Had these students gone directly to a four-year college and maintained a full-time student status, this would have been their first year out of college. These results are discussed in chapter 8, following the stories of our eight students, Allison, Amy, Jerome, Laura, Sam, Seth, Michelle, and Todd.

7

The Realization of Plans

One of the most important questions considered in our longitudinal study centered on the characteristics that influenced the development and realization of students' postsecondary plans. In previous chapters, we considered the effects of parents and family; of students' educational experiences; of peers, teachers, and counselors; and of information. Many theories used in the study of college aspirations and college choice have posited that family background characteristics, especially parental education and income levels, along with student ability, exert a powerful effect on the plans of students. After examining these variables in isolation, we explore how they interact to influence what students actually do upon graduation from high school.

This chapter represents a five-year view of the longitudinal study. It began with 4,923 students and parents. Of the 3,083 respondents to the ninth-grade surveys, 581 students responded to the final survey, which was mailed eight months after the students graduated from high school (a response rate of 18%, the lowest of the eight surveys; return rates declined from a high of 63%, not unusual for longitudinal studies covering a long time frame).

Questions addressed in this chapter relate to the common themes flowing from previous chapters:

- Parental encouragement was the strongest predictor of aspirations in the ninth grade. Did this encouragement translate into college attendance?
- Did parents' education and income have an impact on college attendance?
- Student grade point average had the second strongest impact on educational expectations in the ninth grade. How important was this variable in college attendance?

- What role did peers, teachers, high school counselors, and college admissions counselors play in college attendance? Did their role change over time? Did students have a preference among them?
- Did students' plans become more stable as they moved closer to graduation and matriculation? Among those who went to college, did they attend a college in their consideration set?

PARENTAL ENCOURAGEMENT FOR HIGHER EDUCATION

The parental encouragement variable measured the parents' perception of the amount of encouragement provided to their child. The question asked "How much encouragement have you given your son or daughter to continue his or her education after high school?" Responses were on a Likert-type scale and ranged from "strong encouragement" to "strong discouragement." The student variable measured the student's perception of the amount of encouragement received from parents. While there was a statistically significant difference between the means of these two variables, the means for parent and student variables were high (1.23 and 1.33, respectively). Of students whose parents indicated *giving* strong encouragement, 91 percent reported *receiving* strong encouragement (8% reported receiving "encouragement").

As figure 7.1 illustrates, there was a relationship between parental encouragement and college attendance (nearly 64% of the students receiving strong encouragement attended a four-year institution; and almost 75% receiving strong encouragement attended some form of postsecondary education). A similar pattern exists for those students who received "encouragement" (the second level of parental encouragement).

Twice as many working students received "encouragement" (about 37%) than received "strong encouragement" (about 18%). Students who were encouraged (rather than strongly encouraged) also attended a two-year college at twice the rate (9%) of the strongly encouraged group (4%). The impacts of parental encouragement can also be seen in the type of institution each group attended: nearly 64 percent of the students receiving strong encouragement attended a four-year institution, whereas a little over 39 percent of those merely "encouraged" went to a four-year institution. An explanation for the difference may be students' achievement; parents might have given stronger encouragement to students with better grades. We address this later in the chapter.

Since parental encouragement had such a strong impact on the aspirations of the students in our study, we were not surprised by its impact on the actualization of students' college plans. However, these are simple descriptive statis-

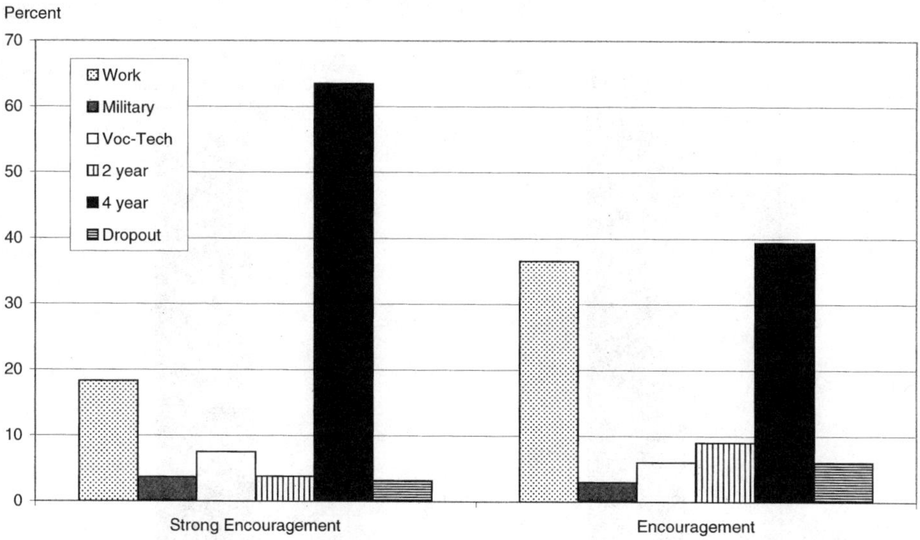

FIGURE 7.1 Influence of Parental Encouragement on Actualized College Plans

tics, which do not always remain significant in more complex predictive models; later in this chapter, we look at a model that does not include the parental encouragement variable. To our surprise, this variable was not significant in the equations for predicting college attendance. Parental encouragement had a significant impact early on, but it became less influential by the senior year, and in the path model for the first year out of high school it was no longer significant. Other background variables (parents' education and income) come to the forefront and have greater impact. Some of our early work with this data set (Hossler and Stage, 1992; Stage and Hossler, 1989), as well as the work of other researchers (Coleman, 1966; Conklin and Daily, 1981), also found parents' education and income to have a direct effect on the college plans of high school students. We offer several logical conclusions regarding the decline in parents' influence.

First, during their junior and senior years, as students became comfortable with the information-gathering process, they moved beyond internal sources to external sources. Second, students' information-processing skills matured along with their natural developmental maturation. As students matured, they wanted to step out beyond the family and gather information on their own. This shift was realized when new information helped the student determine whether the baseline information gathered from internal sources was confirmed or should be modified. The student began to move from novice infor-

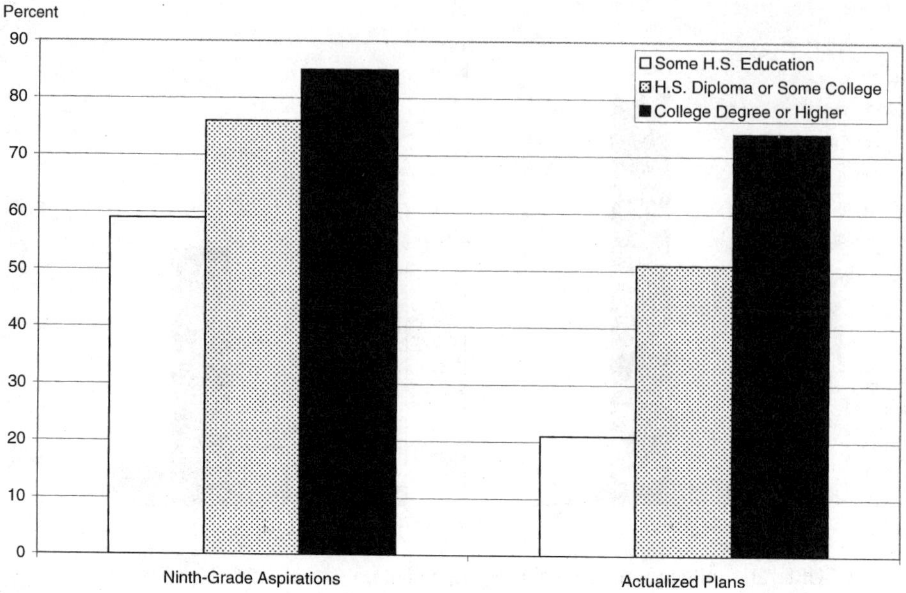

FIGURE 7.2 Influence of Parental Education on Actualized College Plans

mation processor toward expert information processor. Further research may look at the development of information processing in students in the various stages of college choice.

Third, the impact of variables highlighted in other studies, such as parents' education and income, come to the forefront during the latter stages of student college choice. We do not discount the importance of parental encouragement early on in the process, but we do know that the effect of education and income increased during the latter stages of the choice process and that they directly affected the actualization of college plans. While income in particular did not appear to have an effect on student aspirations in the ninth and tenth grades, ultimately, lower levels of income did have a constraining effect on the actualization of students' college plans.

PARENTS' EDUCATION AND INCOME

As reported in earlier chapters, parental education had a direct effect on the college aspirations of ninth-grade students: 59 percent of students whose parents had at least some high school education, 75 percent of students whose parents had a high school diploma or some college, and 86 percent of students whose parents had a college degree or higher. Parents' education had an even

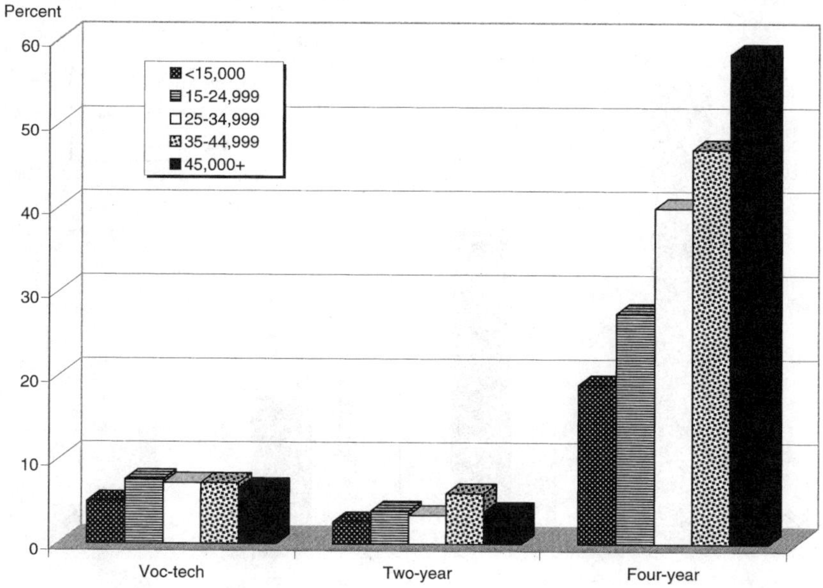

FIGURE 7.3 Influence of Parental Income on Actualized College Plans

greater impact on the actualization of students' college plans. While aspiration levels differed by 11–16 percentage points, actualized plans differed by approximately 25 percentage points (see figure 7.2). Half of the students whose parents had at least a high school diploma attended college, and almost 75 percent whose parents had a college degree attended.

These results suggest that parents' education has a strong effect on the college aspirations of high school students and an even stronger effect on the actualization of their plans. This conclusion is supported by much of the status-attainment literature and reinforces the notion that parents with educational experience provide greater assistance to their children. The higher the level of parental education, the greater the likelihood of their child going to college.

We also measured the relationships between parents' income and both a student's going directly to work after high school and a student's entry into military service. Students from lower-income homes were more likely to go to work: in the three lower-income categories, an average of 20 percent of the students went to work right after high school, compared to an average of 12 percent in the two higher-income categories. These results may be closely linked to parental education, since there is a correlation between educational level and income.

Parental income also had a significant effect on whether students attended vocational schools, technical schools, two-year schools, or four-year schools (see figure 7.3). About 19 percent of the students whose parents' income was below

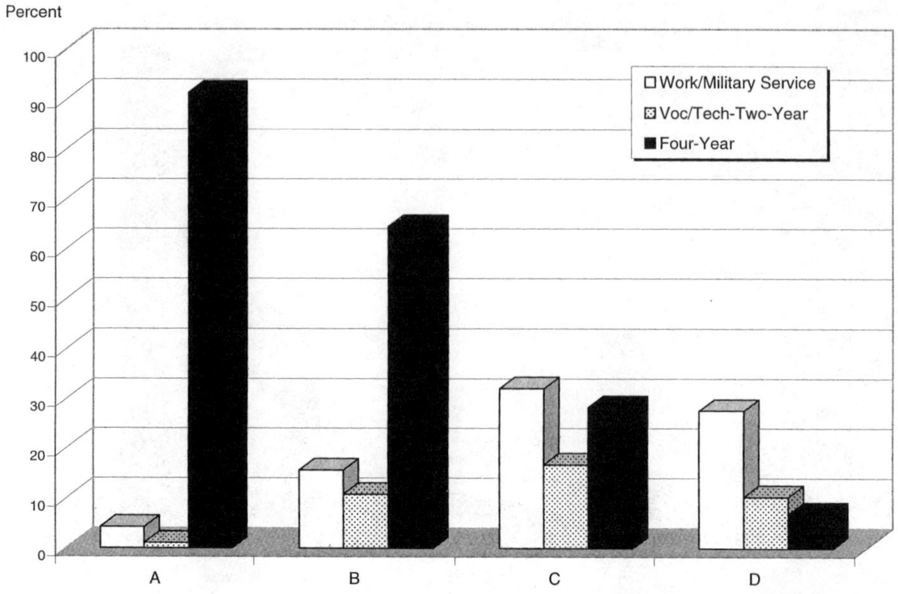

FIGURE 7.4 Influence of Grades in Ninth Grade and Actualized College Plans

$15,000 attended a four-year school, whereas more than 58 percent of the students whose parents' income was more than $45,000 attended a four-year school. While income did not make a difference in student aspirations in the ninth grade, it did have an effect on students' actions five years later.

STUDENT ACHIEVEMENT

In earlier chapters, we identified students' self-reported grade point averages as the second-strongest predictor (after parental encouragement) of college aspirations. With the knowledge of what students actually did their first year out of high school, we can measure the effect of student grades on the actualization of their high school aspirations.

Of the A students, 91 percent attended a four-year college, 4 percent went to work or into military service, and 1 percent attended a vocational or technical school. Of the B students, 65 percent attended a four-year college, and 16 percent went to work or into military service. For students with mostly C's, the numbers begin to change: 32 percent entered the workforce or the military, 17 percent entered a vocational or technical school, and 28 percent attended a four-year college (see figure 7.4).

These results provide a picture consistent with previous research on the predictive nature of grade point average on college attendance. Recall that student grade point average was the second strongest predictor, behind parental encouragement. As mentioned earlier, parental encouragement may be directly related to students' academic achievement: as student grades increase, parents' level of support and their educational expectations increase.

PEERS, TEACHERS, COUNSELORS

The data for this section were derived from a question on one of the twelfth-grade surveys about sources of information a student might use to learn more about colleges. We analyzed the results of students who actually enrolled in college. The question was,

> In the list below are sources of information you might have used to learn more about the colleges or vocational schools which you are considering. Please indicate how helpful each of these sources were as you considered colleges and/or vocational schools.
>
> - Publications and written information sent to you by colleges and vocational schools
> - Talking to counselors
> - Talking to teachers
> - Talking to admissions representatives from colleges
> - Publications and written materials sent to you by the Indiana Career and Postsecondary Advancement Center (ICPAC)
> - Talking to friends
> - Talking to parents and other family members
> - Talking to alumni or currently enrolled students
> - College guide books (*Peterson's Guide*, *Baron's Guide*, etc.)
> - Attending college fairs or college nights

Students were asked to respond to each choice with one of the following: very helpful, helpful, not helpful, and not used.

The results provide a ranking of the information sources used by three groups of students (those attending vocational or technical schools, those attending two-year colleges, and those attending four-year colleges). We combined the "very helpful" and "helpful" categories. The rankings that follow are based on the mean score (in parentheses); a lower score indicates a higher ranking.

1. Publications and written information sent to you by colleges and vocational schools (1.90)

2. Publications and written materials sent to you by ICPAC (1.95)

3. Talking to counselors (2.17)

4. Talking to admissions representatives from colleges (2.18)

5. Talking to teachers (2.25)

6. Talking to parents and other family members (2.41)

7. Talking to alumni or currently enrolled students (2.54)

8. Talking to friends (2.58)

9. College guide books (2.71)

10. Attending college fairs or college nights (3.04)

Colleges should find it encouraging that information they send to students was used most by the students in our sample to learn about those colleges. However, our findings in this area are complex. In our interviews, students consistently told us that they received information from institutions *not* in their consideration set. Many students reported that they "threw away the brochures from colleges not on my list." So while the students ranked information from the colleges and vocational schools as very helpful, we qualify this to include only schools in the student's consideration set. This creates an interesting bind for college admissions professionals. Our interviews suggest that students do not read material from schools they are not interested in, yet students also tell us that written materials from schools they are interested in are useful sources of information.

Another important source of information was ICPAC, a statewide program funded by the state of Indiana to provide postsecondary encouragement for all Indiana students. This center began operation in 1987 and currently provides information to more than 90 percent of Indiana students in grades eight through twelve. The students in our longitudinal study were the same students who were part of the ICPAC pilot program and were recipients of the initial high school postsecondary encouragement campaign. ICPAC information campaigns apparently had an impact, as students ranked ICPAC information as the second most useful source of information about colleges. This finding suggests that state policy makers can play a role in encouraging high school students to continue their education.

The next three resources most used in learning about colleges were high school counselors, high school teachers, and college admissions counselors. As expected, parents ranked in the lower group but above college alumni, currently enrolled students, and friends. The rank of friends is interesting, since so much has been said about students spending more time with their friends than with their family. Apparently, when students are looking for information about colleges they do not look to their friends.

When we looked at only information sources deemed very helpful, we discovered a different order. The same five sources were in the top five spots. Talking to college admissions counselors ranked first and publications and written information sent by colleges was second. These information sources are linked to specific colleges and appear to be viewed as good sources of information about the institutions in the students' consideration sets. The importance of the admissions staff and of college publications is contrasted with the low rankings that college guides and college fairs were given by the students. In all of the comparisons we did, regardless of whether they were attending vocational-technical schools, two-year colleges, or four-year colleges, all groups gave a low ranking to college guides and college fairs. This is curious, since college admissions counselors typically are available to students at college fairs. But students apparently find the admissions counselors more helpful than the fair itself. This may indicate that visits to high schools by college admissions representatives, campus visits in which students have a chance to talk with admissions counselors, and even telephone conversations with students may be more useful ways of reaching students.

The third-ranking very helpful resource was ICPAC information. ICPAC mails grade-based newsletters directly to students' homes and also has a toll-free hotline to answer questions. ICPAC's services have expanded since our survey, so there may be more of an impact on Indiana students today than when ICPAC first started.

The rankings also varied by type of institution attended. Vocational-technical students, two-year-college students, and four-year-college students ranked the same items in the top five but in different orders. Vocational students' top three information sources were publications from the colleges, information from ICPAC, and talking with admissions counselors. Two-year-college students' ranked ICPAC information first, with publications from the colleges second and talking with high school counselors third. Four-year-college students' responses were similar to those of vocational students, with admissions first, ICPAC information second, and a tie for third between high school counselors and teachers.

In summary, the role of significant others changed over the college decision-making process. Of particular interest is the importance of college sources of information. Our earlier results suggested that colleges did not influence choice of college in the latter stages of the process; however, the information they did provide was important. A key role for colleges is in providing detailed information for students already interested in their institutions.

We also found it encouraging that high school counselors and teachers played a larger role when students reached their senior year. Counselors and teachers may want to play larger roles earlier in the process, but they should not ignore the importance of their roles when students reach twelfth grade. Probably the most intriguing finding was the little impact that friends, college guide books, and college fairs had. We do not suggest that these three sources may not be important for some students; however, we saw very little in our survey results to suggest that these sources were helpful in learning about colleges. Finally, the lack of parental impact at this stage is borne out. We recognize that parents have encouraged students throughout the entire process and that parents, teachers, counselors, and even friends may be more encouraging to students who have the grades that indicate educational success—which leads us to the next set of questions.

CONSISTENCY OF PLANS AND ASPIRATIONS

During the eleventh grade, we identified a shift in the stability of students' plans, suggesting that students were more receptive to information about their post–high school options. In this time of exploration, students adjusted their plans as they gathered information from various sources. Whether the plans remained stable is a question addressed in this section.

The ninth-grade survey asked, "What is the highest level of education you expect to achieve?" More than 78 percent of the students reported an interest in some form of education after high school, and approximately 67 percent of graduating seniors in our study enrolled in an educational institution in the year after high school. These college-aspiration figures were later determined to be consistent with the trend in Indiana. ICPAC, which has administered surveys to ninth-grade students in the state for more than ten years, reported similar college-aspiration rates for the state (81%).

We begin by looking at the ninth grade plans and compare them to their plans as sophomores and juniors. The results are discussed for three groups: the going cohort (students who planned to attend school after high school), the not-going cohort (students who planned to stop their formal education after high school), and the undecided cohort (students uncertain about their plans after high school).

The Going Cohort

Of the students who had postsecondary educational aspirations in the ninth grade, 63 percent went on to some form of education after they graduated from high school, 14 percent entered the workforce, and 3 percent entered the military. Of those attending school, 9 percent went to vocational-technical colleges, 8 percent went to two-year colleges, and 84 percent went to four-year colleges. While these figures seem heavily weighted toward the four-year institution, the stratification of institutions in Indiana reflects similar weighting. This may be the result of a lack of a comprehensive statewide community college system.

By the tenth grade, those with college aspirations were even more likely to later actualize their plans. More than 82 percent of tenth-grade students with college aspirations went on to school (compared to 63% of ninth-grade aspirants). Of those students who had postsecondary plans in the tenth grade, 97 percent had the same plans in eleventh grade.

The Not-Going Cohort

The not-going cohort did not follow through on their original post–high school plans to the same degree as the going cohort. Of ninth graders who had plans to work directly after high school, 28 percent did enter the workforce, but 23 percent went to school. Of tenth graders who planned to work the first year out of high school, 44 percent worked but 22 percent attended school. Of ninth graders who planned for military service after high school, 15 percent of them joined the service; however, 29 percent changed their plans and attended school. Of tenth graders with plans to enter the military, 46 percent attended school and 14 percent joined the service. Of those with military plans in tenth grade, 44 percent had those same plans as eleventh graders.

The not-going cohort had the highest high school dropout rate among the three groups (18%, compared to 5% for the going cohort and 12% for the undecided cohort). Those with a plan to enter the military had a high school dropout rate of 12 percent.

The Undecided Cohort

Ninth graders undecided about their post–high school plans demonstrated the greatest variation in actualized plans. Most of these students (36%) attended some type of postsecondary educational institution, some entered the workforce (22%), while others entered military service (4%). Among undecided tenth graders, 55 percent attended school; among undecided eleventh graders, 41 percent attended school. Almost 19 percent of undecided tenth graders remained undecided in eleventh grade. The going cohort was the most likely to follow through on their ninth-grade aspirations. The undecided cohort evidenced the most variability.

Summary

Looking at the actualized plans of students in these three groups, we can see several results. First, the going cohort was the most likely to follow through on their ninth-grade aspirations. Students who were undecided about their plans in ninth grade evidenced the most variability. The most logical explanation for this finding is that undecided students were expressing uncertainty as to what kind of school they planned to attend. However, there may be other explanations. We explore this question later in this chapter. Second, by the senior year, students' aspirations became reliable predictors of what they would actually do. This is useful information for parents, teachers and counselors, and college admissions personnel.

If we look across ninth graders by their plans and actualizations of plans (work, school, and dropping out), we see a direct relationship between aspirations and actualizations. If we assume that those students who dropped out of high school entered the workforce and combine these figures with those who went directly into the workforce, we see a striking relationship between ninth-grade aspirations and actualized plans.

The findings demonstrate that the higher the ninth-grade educational expectation, the greater the likelihood that the expectation will be actualized. The trend across the years was not surprising, in that students begin to stabilize their plans in the twelfth grade and these plans reflect the original plans of the ninth grade. We explore in chapter 8 how these actualized plans suggest great persistence regarding degree completion. Of course, the undecided students did not remain in that category, since later they would be classified as in the workforce, as high school dropouts, or as college students. Much of this chapter suggests that students whose plans shifted between ninth and twelfth grades were less likely to go on to school and were also the most variable.

Of ninth graders who had college plans, 5 percent dropped out of high school; of those who planned to join the military service, 12 percent dropped out; of those who intended to work directly after high school, 18 percent dropped out; of those who were undecided about their post–high school plans, 12 percent dropped out. While students might have returned to one of their options after dropping out of high school, there is clearly a difference among aspirants in their persistence in high school. The difference between the not-going cohort and the undecided cohort was small. Clearly, students who either were uncertain about their plans or did not plan to continue their education after high school are at greater risk of dropping out.

DESTINATIONS

During their junior and senior years in high school, we asked students to list the schools they were considering attending. We were interested in whether the same schools appeared on the lists each year. We also wanted to know if the types of school remained stable from year to year.

From the tenth grade on, there was a good deal of shifting of institutions within a student's consideration set. This is consistent with the shift from internal information sources to external information sources. Nevertheless, 35 percent of students attended a school in their tenth-grade consideration set, and 52 percent attended a school in their eleventh-grade consideration set. Surprisingly, only 62 percent attended a school in their twelfth-grade consideration set. These figures suggest that students make the largest shift toward certainty during their junior year, so this year, when students are most open to options, may be the most opportune time to influence the consideration set.

In the last year of our study, we examined relationships between how students choose their colleges and their satisfaction with these institutions. Using multivariate statistical techniques, we found that students who actively engaged in the search process and who consulted external sources of information were more likely to be satisfied with the college they attended (Hamrick and Hossler, 1995). This finding suggests important linkages between how students investigate their college options and the outcomes of these decisions.

8

What Happened to Our Students?

The information for this chapter came from two phone interviews conducted with students and, on two occasions, with a parent. The first interview occurred one year after the students graduated from high school and the second three years later. These interviews were guided by summaries of transcripts of earlier interviews. In these final interviews, we see the results of four years of planning in high school and, in many cases, four or more years of education. What is most intriguing about these students is the consistency between their plans and what they actually did. If students had clear plans in high school, their actualized plans were consistent four years later. If students were undecided during their high school planning process, they struggled with their plans later. All students had advice for students in high school and their parents.

The chapter begins with a review of the eight students we followed throughout this book. These stories provide the context around which most of this study was based. The last part of the chapter reviews the fifty-six families.

Allison

After spending most of her senior year looking at various career paths and educational options, Allison went to work after graduation. After several months working at the local nursing home, she quit to work at another nursing home. During this first year out of high school, Allison became engaged to be married. She reported being happy with her choices. Allison talked about the support she received from her friends and felt as successful as her friends.

This confidence, however, was not apparent when we talked with Allison three years later. At that time, she was working as a receptionist in a veterinarian's office. Allison did not indicate whether she was still engaged; however, we did not get the impression that she was married. She had worked for two years in the nursing homes and then in a factory on an assembly line, wiring fans and working on heating pads. But she became restless: "after two or three years in the factory, I began looking in the paper and found the receptionist's job in the veterinarian's office."

Allison liked her receptionist's job but was also thinking about going to school. When asked what kind of school, she replied, "I don't know, I haven't thought about it." This statement was similar to many Allison made about plans during her interviews in high school. She continued to struggle with actualizing plans.

In looking back to her ninth-grade year, we can see indications of Allison's lack of clear goals. Allison was the youngest of three daughters. An older sister went to college part-time and eventually graduated, and this sister once provided Allison with information about college. Allison did not have college aspirations in the ninth grade, nor did she have any clear occupational preferences, nor was she involved in high school activities.

In her junior year, Allison's mother reported that Allison "would do nothing at all if she was given the choice" and encouraged Allison to consider joining the military service. There was some discrepancy between the encouragement Allison reported getting from her parents and her parents' perception of their support. On the ninth-grade parent survey, Allison's parents reported being highly encouraging of their daughter's post–high school plans. However, Allison reported that her parents provided no encouragement.

Allison's mother did ask one of her older daughters to get some information for Allison about Lincoln Technical Institute and also reported that Allison was saving money for college. Allison's mother may not have been as encouraging about college as she would have been if she had had more realistic and accurate ideas about the cost of college.

If she had to do it all over again, Allison said, "I probably would have gone to school instead of going to work." Her mother was now encouraging her to go to school and offered to help pay. While Allison had no advice for parents, she did report that her parents had been, and continued to be, supportive. Her advice for students centered on studying: "It's frustrating to study, but do as much as you can or you may end up in a factory"—words from someone who has been there.

Amy

Amy is the student we lost contact with during her junior year in high school. We were unable to contact her for the last two interviews, and the guidance counselor did not know how to locate her. She represents a cohort of students whose difficult circumstances keep them from thinking seriously about their plans after high school. However, we do not have any information on Amy that could guide us in working with others like her.

Jerome

Upon graduation from high school, Jerome attended Vincennes University and completed a two-year degree in general studies. He then transferred to Ball State University to work towards a four-year degree in general studies. In neither case did Jerome mention playing soccer, though playing college soccer was one of his aspirations during his senior-year interviews.

Jerome did not finish at Ball State but transferred to Indiana Wesleyan, a small private college. When asked why he choose Indiana Wesleyan, Jerome was not sure; but his choice of general studies at both Vincennes and Ball State, plus a lack of specific careers goals, could indicate he was searching for the right school to fit his needs. When asked what advice he had for students, Jerome replied, "to learn study skills in high school." In the ninth-, eleventh-, and twelfth-grade surveys, Jerome reported C grades, so his reason for transferring may be that his college courses were difficult. Jerome's mother once commented on his grades: "I looked at his grades—B's, C's, and D's—and told him he was not ready for a big place like IU [Indiana University]."

Another comment from an earlier interview suggests an economic reason for changing schools. Jerome's parents paid for the first two years of college (at Vincennes) but did not help financially after he completed his associate's degree. In his interview during his junior year in high school, Jerome indicated that he did not expect to pay any of his college costs. He expected his parents to pay and to get financial aid if needed. However, his mother did not want him to take out loans. At the time of the last interview, Jerome had been working as a furnace installer for two years and was going to school part-time.

Jerome was the middle child of three boys, active in athletics, and according to his mother did not have friends "of the college nature." He may have struggled from a lack of career focus. In the ninth grade, he had aspirations for a four-year degree but did not indicate any occupational or academic interest area. By his junior year, Jerome had a variety of career interests: law, dentistry, police work. In the spring of his junior year he wanted to major in business management or criminology. Jerome seemed confused about what to study in college. In his junior year, he recalled his father (who owned a taxi business) telling him "not to work in this business." His mother, a music teacher, told him that she did not want him to be a teacher. She also clearly wanted him to attend college in the state. Since he did not know what he wanted, since his friends were not college bound, and since his parents were not recommending the fields they were in, Jerome may have struggled with the purpose of college attendance.

Jerome ended his interview with a suggestion for parents, recommending that they "not rely on teachers" but "encourage and motivate" their children. His parents had been supportive during the first two years of college, at least financially, and did try to talk with him about his post–high school plans. But his mother once remarked that "they don't necessarily want help; they like to do things on their own," and this may reflect the direction that Jerome's parents' efforts took.

Laura

Laura went to the University of Southern Indiana after she graduated from high school but dropped out after one semester. She worked in the spring semester, mostly full-time, at a fast-food restaurant, work she did not like. She then found a job as a receptionist at a hair salon, which she enjoyed. Laura had signed up for a class at Purdue University at Anderson but dropped the class because she did not like it. She was now considering dental hygiene classes at IUPUI. Laura's father was involved in her educational plans, as he was during high school. "My father is checking out the school [IUPUI] now," she said, "and has made several calls. He gets excited about what he finds out for me." At this time, however, Laura had not applied to any school.

Four years later, Laura reported that she did enroll in the dental hygiene program at IUPUI. She had completed her associate's degree, had taken the national board exam, and was waiting to take the state board exam. She expected to be "employed in a dental office" shortly after that. She did not consider IUPUI a "normal college; it is more of a commuter college." Her parents paid for the first two years, and she took out a loan to finance her last semester.

According to her ninth-grade survey, Laura had plans to attend college and obtain a four-year degree. She was a B student in ninth grade but was not as academically talented as her older sister, who attended Hanover College, a private college in Indiana. Laura had indicated an interest in Ball State University as early as the tenth grade, and this was where she began her college career.

If she had to do it all over again, Laura said she "would not have gone to Ball State or roomed with my friend." Her advice to high school students was "to enjoy it while you can, because college is not like high school," noting that "it is more difficult to meet people once you get out" of high school.

Laura had not kept up with high school friends but felt she did better in school than her friends. Her advice to parents was to "make sure your children are taking classes to prepare them for graduation."

Laura had the most controlling father of the eight students we followed but did not reflect any resentment about his involvement in her planning activities. This is particularly interesting since her parents were frank about the deficiencies they saw in their daughter. At times during her earlier interviews, Laura mentioned going "far away from home" and recognized that she would not be free if she stayed at home. She did attend college near her home, however, and seemed happy with her choice.

Sam

Sam, our most informed and motivated college aspirant, attended Eckerd College in Florida and was satisfied with his choice. He decided not to pursue engineering as a major but finished all four years at Eckerd. Most of the schools Sam had considered throughout his high school search process included engineering schools. His decision to attend Eckerd was consistent with his search for engineering schools, since he had the option of going to Eckerd for three years and then transferring to another Florida school to complete two more years for a degree in engineering.

Sam was very involved in college. He was in choir and in theater; he helped with the homeless and tutored other students through the Cornerstone Club, a Christian club he helped found. He reported that he "had to study a lot more, especially my freshman year." Sam was the most informed student of the eight but then made a college choice that seemed idiosyncratic. His other choices were Massachusetts Institute of Technology, Purdue University, Rose-Hulman Institute of Technology, and California Institute of Technology.

He did receive a scholarship, which paid for over half his expenses, but he recommended that parents "be sure and save up some money, because that kind of makes choices easier." Sam graduated with a double major in physics and math and planned to find a teaching job in Florida. Sam is "happy to be done with school," but if he had to do it over again, he would have looked into a Bible college.

Sam was a first-generation college student. His sister had died, so he was an only child. He was an A student in high school and had ninth-grade plans to attend college and to obtain a graduate degree. In high school, he was moderately active in athletics and his church groups. His early occupational interests were physical sciences, math, computer science, management, and business. Sam finished his college career having done much of what he anticipated on his ninth-grade survey. His parents were supportive throughout the entire process of his search and during his four years in college, and he recommended that parents continue to support their college children and to keep in touch with them.

Seth

Seth attended Vincennes University and was satisfied with his choice. He estimated that he studied six to ten hours a week and completed most of his homework on time. He was not involved in college life outside of intramural athletics and in his freshman year had not been sure that his parents could afford his second year of college. Seth lived in the residence hall and became a resident assistant during his second year. The primary reason for becoming an RA may have been financial.

Three years later, we found that Seth had been promoted from resident assistant to hall manager. Upon graduating from Vincennes, he had transferred to Purdue University, where he was a residence hall counselor. The transition took some adjustment. "It was a shock to go from a school of 6,000 to one of 36,000. The maximum number of students in a class at Vincennes was fifty; sometimes here [at Purdue] it is three or four hundred."

Seth completed his associate's degree at Vincennes in wildlife management and at Purdue was majoring in fisheries and aquatic science. "I changed over for a couple of reasons. One, there's no jobs, and sort of secondly, because I didn't like the classes, you know, business classes, which I haven't got a clue how to do." Seth was happy with the way his plans had actualized but added these thoughts about his high school preparation: "I could have been [better] prepared by taking college credit courses in high school. In college, I had to take a lot of introductory courses in chemistry, algebra, and other courses because I had never been introduced to that kind of stuff." Seth's recommendation for high school students was to get the most out of their courses.

In the ninth grade, Seth's grades were B's and C's. He was active in athletics and aspired to obtain a vocational degree. His occupational interests were mechanical engineering, industrial production work, and hospitality work. His top two majors at that time were engineering and fine arts. Both his occupational interests and major interests are a contrast to fisheries and aquatic science.

The most interesting part of Seth's story relates to parental support. During the ninth grade, Seth's parents did not think they would need any financial assistance to send him to school. By the tenth grade, they thought they might need some financial assistance. During the junior year, Seth's father reported he had been saving for his son's college expenses for three to five years. And by his senior year, Seth's parents thought they could pay for 75 percent of college costs, since Seth had selected a low-cost school. However, during Seth's first year at Vincennes, he was not sure if his parents could afford the second year. Perhaps a financial crisis in the family prompted Seth to search for other financing options. Perhaps the residence hall position filled this need.

When asked how his parents had supported him during this process, he said, "they encouraged me to go to college, they helped me get college information, and my mother worked at the school cafeteria and would let me know when the college representatives were going to visit the school. They also took me on campus visits and provided funds for my college costs." Seth consistently reported support from his parents throughout the entire study.

Michelle

Michelle planned to attend Oakwood College during the latter part of her senior year. Oakwood is a religiously affiliated school, similar to Andrews University, which was also in her consideration set during her junior year. She attended Oakwood for one year but did not return since it was "too far away from home." Michelle planned to "sit out for a year and work" but did say that Oakwood was a good school. Like many of our students, she was able to judge schools better after she had attended. After saying that Oakwood was a good school, she qualified it by saying that it was "not a top one, since sometimes I had to use the library at Alabama A&M, down the road."

Michelle made the honor roll at Oakwood, continuing to improve her academic record: in the ninth grade Michelle reported mostly C grades but by eleventh grade was receiving mostly B's. Although she did not return after an academically successful year at Oakwood, Michelle said, "I wouldn't trade my year in Alabama for anything." She did talk about being far from home, "but it was my first time away from home, which was kind of hard."

Three years later, we found that Michelle had a two-year-old child. She had attended Indiana Business College (IBC, which had been on her senior consideration set) but had completed only ten months of an eighteen-month program. She quit because her son was too young for her to leave him. Michelle was a single parent and "would have finished at IBC if I had not had my baby."

Michelle had college aspirations as a ninth grader and wanted to obtain a four-year degree. She had fallen short of that goal at this time but had pursued a practical degree. Her occupational interest areas in the ninth grade were in business, with major interests in math, business, and computers. Her course of study at IBC was consistent with these early aspirations.

We also clearly see the impact of parental involvement with Michelle, who was the youngest of three children and the only daughter. In her junior year, Michelle's mother reported that Michelle wanted "to go to a school close to home. She's not sure right now. She doesn't want to leave me now. But once she gets out of high school, it may be a whole new ball game." During this period, Michelle was interested in exploring historically black colleges: "I read about a couple of them and talked to a friend about it. His family went to an all-black college, and I was like, *Yes!*, that is what I want! Then I thought about it. Was I looking to the right things? I really need a book that tells you about it, and the only college I have talked to is Andrews. I want to go to an all-black college in the South, but I just haven't talked to them or gotten any information yet." By her senior year in high school, Michelle planned to go to IBC, which her mother thought was a good idea: "You get courses specifically related to what you want to do. Also, they offer refresher courses. . . . She can always finish her four-year degree later, if she wants to."

Michelle now works at GTE North as a sales representative. Previous to this job, she worked at a shopping mall as a sales clerk. She talked about the possibility of going back to finish her IBC program if she could get some grants. "I can't afford the cost on my own, right now." This concern for finances was also a concern in our early interviews with Michelle. During the eleventh-grade interviews, she said that financial aid would affect her decision, "because I don't have a lot of money."

Michelle had been on the honor roll at IBC, she has competed academically and enjoyed the time spent in college, and we think she will return some day and finish what she started.

Todd

After high school, Todd followed his dream to hike the Appalachian Trail. He injured his ankle several times during the hike, and only made half of the two-thousand-mile trip. He planned to return some day to hike the remaining miles.

Todd went to work after the hiking trip and had a few "not so serious" jobs. He was now working at the factory where his brother worked. Todd had been promoted to inspector and was happy with this advancement. His brother was also an inspector. Todd made no mention of further education and said that he was "brought up to go to work."

Todd got married about a two and a half years after high school and had one child and two stepchildren. His advice for young people was "do not give up, because it will all come together sooner or later." Todd also thought that "a high school diploma will get you a long way. For those who go to work after high school, there is better than fast-food."

While Todd did not pursue any education after high school, he provides an example of a student who set goals and was happy with his achievements. Todd reported having a lot of encouragement from his parents: "They let me make my own decisions. Through experiences they had, they tried to help me, since parents will always have more experience than their children. They also try to pass on some of that wisdom. . . . Just believe in and trust your children, and they'll succeed at something one time or another. You got to stick with them and help them along."

In the ninth grade, Todd had no aspirations for formal education beyond high school and was only considering military service. His brother had entered the service, but Todd's eyesight kept him from his goal. Todd had mostly C grades in high school. His mother had completed some college, his father had completed high school. Todd was one of the most goal-oriented students in our study who had no plans for further education after high school.

THE FIFTY-SIX FAMILIES

During the students' eleventh-grade year, three cohorts were generated for students from eight high schools who had completed the ninth-grade survey. Fifty-six families were selected from these cohorts, which were based on the survey question that asked about the highest level of education students expected to achieve. Students who selected vocational-technical certification, two-year college degrees, four-year college degrees, master's degrees, or professional degrees were placed in the "going" cohort; student who selected a high-school diploma were placed in the "not-going" cohort; students who were undecided were placed in the "undecided" cohort.

The primary rationale for the three cohorts relates to the college-choice process. If students are not going to pursue any educational options after high school, then they are not likely to be involved in the search stage of college choice. Therefore, we would have different kinds of questions for this cohort. However, we included this group in our study because ninth graders are not locked into this decision and could choose to pursue educational options while in our study. The same would be true for the undecided cohort.

The Going Cohort

Twenty students were part of the going cohort for whom we have data across the eight years. All twenty students actualized their plans to go on to school the first year out of high school. Seventeen of them graduated, fifteen from a four-year institution, two from a two-year institution. This graduation rate (85%) is surprising and generates many questions about the search and choice stages of the decision-making process and about the effect choice of college has on persistence rate.

Of the twenty students, eighteen had four-year-degree aspirations in the ninth grade, two had two-year-degree aspirations. Of the eighteen four-year-degree aspirants, fourteen graduated from a four-year institution, one attended a two-year institution and received her associate's degree, one earned certificates in cosmetology and pharmacy technology, and two attended college for two years and dropped out. Both of the students interested in a two-year institution received associate's degrees; one of them went on to graduate from a four-year institution.

These results suggest that students with college plans as early as ninth grade gain information-processing and decision-making skills that contribute to college persistence. Many students planning to attend college after high school talked about information-gathering activities and provided many indicators of critical thinking about the decisions before them. They were faced with many decisions during the course of their high school career, including attending camps, taking achievement tests, sending away for information, and visiting campuses. We theorize that these information-processing and decision-making experiences built confidence, which they used to make a myriad of decisions in college.

The stability of the postsecondary plans of this cohort through their high school years was strong. Only one of the twenty aspirants changed plans from ninth to tenth grades, from planning to go to a two-year school to "undecided," in which category he remained until his senior year, when he returned to the two-year-college category. He completed his associate's degree and went on to earn a four-year degree. Another student changed her plans by twelfth grade; she attended college for a couple of years and then dropped out. By the first year out of high school, three more students had changed their plans. One never attended a four-year institution but studied cosmetology and pharmacy. The other student, who had been active in Future Farmers of America (FFA) in high school, served as a state officer in FFA his first year out of high school. He went to college the following year, finishing a four-year program in three and a half years. The other student attended college for two years and then dropped out.

In summary, only three of the twenty students deviated from their ninth-grade college plans. The results suggest that plans for college-bound ninth graders are stable across time, a stability that may extend into college.

The Not-Going Cohort

There were six students, for whom we have eight years of data, who indicated in the ninth grade that they did not have plans to pursue an education beyond high school. Of the six, four did not attend any formal educational institution after high school and so were consistent with their ninth-grade aspirations. This consistency is similar to that of the going cohort. Of the two students who attended college, one graduated from a two-year institution and transferred to a four-year institution. The other attended two semesters and then dropped out.

While the final plans of the not-going cohort were the same as their original aspirations (for five of the six), the stability of plans across the years changed, mostly between the tenth and eleventh grades.

The Undecided Cohort

During the first four years of this study, it was theorized that students in the undecided category might go to college but were simply undecided as to level of education. Since the survey question did not allow for multiple responses, this was a logical hypothesis. The results reveal a much different story. Six of the eleven students who were undecided about their postsecondary plans graduated from college, five from four-year institutions, one from a two-year institution. Of the five students who did not graduate from college, two attended college their first year out of high school but dropped out and were now working; two went to work right out of high school; one went into military service.

The undecided cohort had a less stable pattern than the going cohort. In tenth grade, two formerly undecided students thought they would go to college after high school; by eleventh grade, six more made such plans. Possibly, even in the ninth grade these undecided students were planning to attend college but were undecided as to the level. By the twelfth grade, ten of the eleven students who were undecided in the ninth grade had postsecondary educational plans (the other student enlisted in the military service).

Between grade twelve and one year out, three students had decreased their college aspirations; between the first year out and the fourth year out, two students had reduced theirs, and two had increased theirs. These results show a lack of stability in the plans of undecided students. This cohort may respond most to the interventions of teachers and high school counselors.

Summary

These results point to the consistency of ninth-grade plans. We did not suggest at the onset of this study that ninth-grade students would follow through on plans made so early in their high school careers. Common descriptors of ninth graders include self-centeredness, immaturity, and a preoccupation with trivial aspects of themselves. However, in this study, ninth graders appeared to think seriously about their postsecondary plans and followed through with significant consistency. This was the case for both the going cohort and the not-going cohort. The undecided cohort certainly remained undecided until later in their high school career; however, once plans were made in the eleventh grade, that pattern of consistency remained for the following two years.

Another common theme throughout the interviews for all three groups was the increased activity during the eleventh grade and the first part of the twelfth grade. While aspirations remained constant for the going cohort, activity increased during this time period, when these students may have been involved in the interactive search phase (Schmit, 1991). Interactive search involves sending for and responding to information from colleges, sending for and completing financial aid forms, and continuing to explore career options. This period appears to be an optimal time for institutions to communicate with students (even though most students reported reading information only from colleges in their consideration sets and discarding information from schools not in their set). This finding, however, is still good news for colleges who focus on the early years of high school in their recruitment efforts.

CONCLUSION

The most consistent remark from students who attended college was regarding the difference between college-level work and high school–level work. Most students recommended that students in high school make the best of the time they had and to take courses that would prepare them for college-level work.

Concern about college costs and financial aid options was present from the beginning of the study (ninth grade) for parents but seemed less important for students until they were in the later stages of the decision-making process.

These concerns varied greatly and speak to a need to inform parents and students early about their college-financing options.

Finally, the importance of parents in the college-choice process continued to be evident. Level of involvement varied, but parental interest was apparent throughout the larger study. Almost all of the students we contacted in the eight years of the study mentioned the importance of parental encouragement. And all of the parents indicated an interest in their children's happiness.

The concluding chapter provides a summary of the entire study and recommendations for the many groups interested in the student college-choice process.

Conclusion

In 1995, we had the opportunity of hosting several visiting university professors from Russia. These Russian educators expressed an interest in learning more about career planning offices and vocational guidance programs in high schools and colleges. Since perestroika and the end of centralized economic planning in the former Soviet Union, the connections between postsecondary education and employment had unraveled. High school and university graduates were no longer guaranteed a job. In the new market economy, they also did not know how to find jobs. The Russian educators held the understandable belief that vocational and career planning programs could fix this problem.

To our Russian friends, the transition from U.S. high schools to work or college appeared seamless. The complexities and outcomes of the countless decisions that students and their parents make were not visible to those who had not been through the process. Each year in the United States, close to three million high school seniors graduate (*Digest of Educational Statistics*, 1996). Following countless graduation ceremonies, they make the formal transition from compulsory education to a life filled with noncompulsory decisions. Any reflective parent with high school children, the students themselves, their teachers and counselors, and college admissions personnel are well aware that postsecondary career and educational decisions are anything but simple; they are, instead, the complex products of cumulative decisions and experiences.

In this chapter, we highlight our findings and what they mean for parents, high school teachers and counselors, college policy makers, and public policy makers. We also speculate on fruitful areas for additional research.

In the introduction to this volume, six questions were identified as the primary purposes of this study. While we return to five of these questions, we do so with the realization that the answers are much more complicated than we realized at the outset of this investigation. The questions are

1. How do students develop college aspirations? How do their plans evolve and change over time?

2. How and when do students find out about colleges?

3. How do students choose colleges?

4. How do tuition costs and financial aid influence the college decision-making process?

5. Do students achieve their college aspirations, and what factors affect whether they do?

THE FINDINGS

One of our most important findings is the difference between the factors that influence students' aspirations and those that influence their achievements. The influences on the college decisions of ninth-grade students are different from the influences on the decisions of twelfth-grade students.

Factors in the Predisposition Stage

Most high school students develop stable postsecondary plans by the time they complete the ninth grade. By the fall after their high school graduation, more than 60 percent of students in our sample followed through on the plans they expressed in the ninth grade. Nearly 70 percent of students followed through on their tenth-grade plans. The educational aspirations of most sophomores and juniors actually increased after ninth grade. More than half of students who were undecided about their postsecondary plans in the ninth grade planned, by their junior year, to continue their formal education after high school. Nevertheless, students whose plans changed between ninth and twelfth grades were less likely to go to college. Although the plans of many students were still evolving, there is little doubt that the best time to influence their postsecondary plans is during or even before their first year of high school.

The findings from this study also demonstrate that parents play the key role in shaping the early plans of students. Consistently, we found that students who reported talking more to their parents about their plans and who reported that their parents encouraged their college plans were likely to plan to continue their formal education beyond high school. The important role that parents play is documented in reviews of the research on student college choice (Hossler, Braxton, and Coopersmith, 1989; Paulsen, 1990). We also found that parents' educational level, student achievement (as measured by grade point average), the influence of peers, and involvement of students in high school organizations and activities have an impact on the predisposition stage.

Factors in the Search Stage

As early as tenth grade, many students could name one or more colleges they were considering attending after high school. Since tenth graders talked most to parents about their postsecondary plans, we postulate that parents played a key role in identifying these institutions. For Jerome, Laura, and Michelle, their parents and older siblings helped them identify specific colleges. Sam, Seth, Allison, and Michelle also learned about schools from high school staff, from church members, and from printed information about schools.

Sophomores, more than juniors, were certain about the characteristics of colleges and universities that were important to them (size, cost, academic selectivity), but they were less involved in learning more about specific schools. Neither ninth or tenth graders were interested in financial aid information, but the parents of ninth graders were interested in financial aid information and tuition costs. Overall, sophomores were actively engaged in the search stage of the college decision-making process.

During the eleventh grade, students who were planning to attend college became more actively engaged in gathering information. Increasingly during their junior and senior years students also moved beyond their parents, siblings, and peers as they sought information about colleges and universities. They instead sought information from teachers, guidance counselors, and college admissions personnel. They also wrote to colleges to request information, to read college guidebooks, and to visit college campuses. The time period during which students are most actively involved in learning about colleges extends from late in the junior year through early in the senior year.

Factors in the Choice Stage

How students choose among colleges proved a difficult question to answer. Throughout our research, we asked students what schools they were considering attending. Furthermore, in an attempt to identify a pattern in type of school students chose, one year after high school graduation we asked them which school they had attended. Our goal was to see how stable students' consideration sets were over time. We also wanted to uncover relationships between student characteristics and experiences and the types of school they considered and ultimately attended.

The type of school students considered were remarkably stable over time.

The admissions selectivity and costs of colleges in students' consideration sets had high degrees of consistency from the tenth grade to the twelfth grade. In addition, the cost and selectivity of the schools that students attended were consistent with those of the schools they were considering throughout high school. However, the specific schools changed throughout the high school years.

Each year we asked students how important particular college characteristics were and found that students were more certain about important characteristics in their sophomore and senior years than they were as juniors. In addition, during the junior year, students considered the largest number of schools, and sophomores and seniors had the fewest number of schools in their consideration sets.

Based upon these results, we posit the following. High school sophomores who plan to attend college are already considering specific schools and even have some idea about the qualities they are looking for in a school. However, high school graduation and college attendance are still in the distant future, and sophomores are not actively gathering information about their options and are not making serious plans.

During their junior year, students begin to realize that this decision is no longer in the distant future. They begin to gather information and learn about specific schools. As a result, they become less certain instead of more certain of their plans; as they learn more about schools, new questions arise, and they become less certain about what they are looking for in a career or college. Juniors also learn about schools they had not heard of before and add some of them to their consideration sets, as they drop other schools. Thus, the junior year is a period of uncertainty and exploration. Furthermore, high-ability students are even more uncertain about which college characteristics are important, and their consideration sets are large. Seniors narrow the size of their consideration sets and become more certain about the institutional characteristics important to them. Nevertheless, high-ability seniors continue to have larger consideration sets and are often less certain about what they are looking for in a college.

Our results reveal a high degree of consistency over time in students' consideration sets. Using multivariate statistical techniques, we found that students whose consideration sets included schools with similar tuition costs or admissions selectivity had higher grade point averages and, during their senior year, talked more frequently with peers, teachers, counselors, and alumni—and less with parents. These students were also more involved in searching for information and institutions. We posit that higher grades and more external sources of information are mutually reinforcing. Students who earn better grades also talk to high school personnel more about their plans, and they receive more college marketing literature.

The influence of external sources reaches its peak from late in the junior year to early in the senior year. There is scant evidence that external sources of information affect students' ninth- and tenth-grade consideration sets. In the eleventh grade, however, 95 percent of students engaged in some form of external information gathering. By the twelfth grade, students were even more actively gathering information, and in addition, 60 percent of seniors said that college material they had received in the mail had either a "great influence" or "some influence" on which school they planned to attend. Of course, more than half of the respondents also said that such mail had little or no impact on their choice of college. However, college mail marketing has some influence on students' evaluations of the schools in their consideration sets and also in their matriculation decisions.

Financial Factors

High school students are not generally interested in either college tuition costs or student financial aid until their senior year. Throughout their ninth, tenth, and eleventh grades (and even to some extent, their twelfth grade), students conveyed an attitude that financing their education was the responsibility of their parents. On the other hand, as early as when their children were in ninth grade, parents indicated that they were interested in information about college costs and financial aid.

Both high school seniors and their parents were well informed about financial aid programs and their eligibility for financial aid. More than 70 percent of parents and students were either "very well informed" or "informed" about college costs. More than 50 percent of parents were informed about federal and state financial aid programs. Given that not all respondents expected to be eligible for financial aid, this is a relatively high percentage. More than 63 percent of parents and 70 percent of seniors were either "very certain" or "certain" that the parents would be able to pay for schooling. The more of the costs students expected their parents to pay, the more certain both students and parents were that the parents would be able to pay for schooling.

In the November twelfth-grade survey, we asked parents to estimate the influence of financial aid on the advice they would offer to their children about which institution they should attend. We asked students a similar question. Parents' responses revealed that a small amount of financial aid ($500 to $1,000) could exert a modest influence on their advice and that moderate-sized awards ($1,001 to $3,000) could have a strong influence. Half of the students said that a financial aid award could have "some" effect or a "strong" effect on their matriculation decision, and half believed that an award would have a "small" effect or "no" effect. No specific dollar amount was specified in the question asked students.

Unfortunately, our findings are more complex when the results from our interviews are included. During most of our interviews, both parents and students said that financial aid alone would not have that much effect on matriculation decisions. Some researchers (Jackson, 1982; Freeman, 1984; Hossler and Bean, 1990) have reported that relatively small amounts of financial aid, when used in conjunction with a comprehensive recruitment strategy, can have a significant impact on student enrollment decisions. Other studies (Chapman and Jackson, 1987; Moore, Studenmundt, and Slobko, 1991) have found that it takes large financial aid awards to influence students' matriculation decisions. Several of these studies, however, were conducted only with high-ability students; our study included a broad range of student abilities.

Factors in the Actualization Stage

The most important factor in whether students went to college was strong support and encouragement from their parents. The outcome was not strongly associated with parental education or income, suggesting that family social and economic status was not a key determinant.

All twenty students in the going cohort of the fifty-six-family subsample attended college, and seventeen of the twenty had graduated by the time of the last interview. Of the eleven students in the undecided cohort, six graduated from some type of postsecondary school, two had taken some classes but had not graduated, one had entered military service, and two were working. Of the six students in the not-going cohort, four were working and two had taken some postsecondary courses. These findings show that if we expand the length of time for our analysis, most students do actualize their plans. Caution needs to be exercised in the interpretation of these results. Our fifty-six-family subsample is dramatically smaller than the survey sample, and as a result we cannot use sophisticated statistical procedures. In addition, it is possible that the constant attention and exchange of information that took place between the research team and the participants influenced students' decisions.

Some Conclusions

Throughout the study, we compared the findings from the survey data with those from the interview data and discovered a high degree of concordance. This leads us to the tentative conclusion that we would have discovered similar patterns for the entire sample had we been able to survey them in the spring and summer of 1994.

Operating on this assumption, we offer the following explanations of our findings. As students move closer to high school graduation they (and their parents) learn more about postsecondary educational options. In addition, gaps between their hoped-for academic performance and the realities become more evident, and the effects of these gaps become more concrete. Lower grades result in students receiving less parental, teacher, and counselor support and encouragement and less information about postsecondary education. During the junior and senior years, parents and students become more knowledgeable about college costs and financial aid. For some families, this means that concerns about paying for college become more pronounced. Other barriers may also begin to emerge for students whose parents have only a high school education or lack financial resources. They might find it difficult to make multiple campus visits, to seek private college counseling, or simply to purchase guidebooks and other resources. Like one of the students we profiled in this study, many of these students may not know "how to get there from here."

Students in the twelfth grade have smaller and less diverse consideration sets than students in the eleventh grade. We posit that, as students in their junior year learn more about specific schools and specific college characteristics, they entertain more educational options. However, in their senior year the realities of costs, selectivity, and such factors as distance from home become prominent again. By the senior year, parents have played a key, if subliminal role, in establishing the constraints on students' consideration sets. Comments like "we can't afford that," "there are plenty of good in-state public universities," or "we will help you to attend any school you want to enter," which may have been said to students in the eighth, tenth, or even fifth grades, do much to determine both student's consideration sets and their enrollment decisions.

These explanations do not mean that students cannot break out of the limitations set by their parents or by economic, social, and academic constraints, nor do they mean that the information gathering of students or the marketing activities of colleges do not have an effect. Clearly, they do. However, the effect of teachers, counselors, and admissions offices on the outcomes of the college decision-making process is limited.

IMPLICATIONS AND RECOMMENDATIONS

Parents

Parents play the most significant role in shaping the educational aspirations of their children. Their education or income levels are not important determinants, but their encouragement and support of their children are. Parents should communicate high educational expectations to their children when they are young; it is likely that students who aspire to go on to college have never considered not doing so, because since they were young their parents have said such things as "a high school diploma is not enough," or "of course, you will go to college," or "don't worry about paying for college, somehow we'll find the money."

Another important way that parents can communicate their expectations and support is by starting a college savings account. No matter how small the amount, students interpret parental savings as a tangible commitment. Parents can also express their support and encouragement by assisting their children as they search for information about colleges and as they evaluate their consideration sets. By taking their children on campus visits and by attending financial aid workshops, parents convey support for students' college aspirations. And parents can serve as sounding boards as their children explore specific educational institutions.

Rogoff (1990) has suggested that parents play six roles important for cognitive development: (1) stimulating children's interest in cognitive tasks, (2) simplifying tasks so children can manage them, (3) motivating children and providing direction to their activities, (4) giving feedback, (5) controlling frustration and risk, and (6) demonstrating idealized versions of the acts to be performed. The application of Rogoff's six points to the student college-choice process has some interesting possibilities.

Several questions are raised based on the themes developed in the parental involvement framework. Can the framework be marked by time frames similar to the stages of college choice? Can the components be described to parents in such a way as to reduce the stress of this life decision for students? Once parents recognize components that assist students in their decision-making process, the process may provide a great learning tool for students and their parents. Finally, how can colleges help parents understand the college-choice process? Can they provide parents with a comprehensive view of the decision-making process and the important role they, as parents, play in it? The role of parents is a vital one, and schools have no resource more committed to and vested in the outcomes.

High School Teachers and Counselors

As early as junior high school, teachers and counselors should provide structured experiences for students to learn about their college options. The ratio of students to counselors is too high for personal counseling to be a viable strategy for working with students. Thus, group counseling or using course assignments to encourage students to gather college information would be useful. Programs designed to assist students during the summer between their junior and senior years would be especially helpful. Teachers and counselors can also provide academic support programs. Academic success in high school is linked to actualizing educational plans.

Teachers and counselors help form students' consideration sets. We submit that it is advantageous for students to consider a wide range of schools, but teachers and counselors are limited by their own experience in helping students enlarge these sets. Further, many high school guidance counselors have had little training in college counseling and need professional development opportunities to learn more about college counseling. We lack empirical data, but it is our impression that teachers and counselors often cannot help students understand the differences among various types of college. Students with extensive sources of external information, including teachers and counselors, are more likely to actualize their college plans.

Teachers and counselors can also help educate parents and students about financial aid programs. Parents express an interest in such information as early as their children's freshman year in high school. By the eleventh grade, parents have a strong demand for such information.

College Admissions Personnel

Our findings suggest that college admissions personnel do not have a strong personal and direct impact upon the matriculation decisions of students. However, printed information has some effect upon students' decisions. A few students are ready to read information from colleges as early as their sophomore year, but these students are rare. During their junior year, students report receiving and reading more information. Generally, all of their information-gathering activities increase. Our research cannot provide detailed insights into the kinds of information that students prefer or when they are most likely to make use of information. It is clear, however, that students demonstrate the most intense levels of information gathering between the spring of their junior year and the fall of their senior year. It may be wise for college admissions personnel to provide only brief information to sophomores and first-semester juniors.

Admissions personnel should also develop marketing efforts designed for parents. Parents set the parameters on the kinds of institution students consider. Financial aid and college cost information should be directed at parents; they are the decision makers with respect to tuition and financial aid. This recommendation is awkward because, from a developmental perspective, admissions and financial aid personnel try to involve prospective students directly as part of students' preparation for adulthood. However, in financial areas, parents are the main decision makers.

Financial aid awards can make a difference in college choice. While our data cannot provide definitive information on the impact of aid awards, perceptual information suggests that for students considering less expensive public institutions, modest financial aid awards could influence their enrollment decisions.

Public Policy Makers

The results of this study suggest that community, regional, and statewide efforts to provide information about postsecondary education options, costs, and financial aid could be beneficial for students and parents. For such efforts, timing is everything. Parents of young children and early adolescents should be the focus of early-awareness college programs. Parents shape the aspirations of their children and are far more interested than students in information about college costs and financial aid.

Although we lack enough data to make strong assertions, it is our sense that early-awareness programs should provide simple and brief information. Neither the parents of young children nor the children themselves are ready for detailed information about how to apply to college or to state scholarship programs. Information should be designed to stimulate further interest. Efforts like the Indiana Career and Postsecondary Advancement Center could provide a model for state public policy makers.

Of course, academic support programs would also help students to achieve their goals. Academic success in high school is linked to the likelihood that students will achieve their educational goals. Thus, any efforts that help students to succeed academically will also help them realize their educational goals.

Community, regional, and state policy makers should design information strategies for high school juniors and seniors and their parents. At this stage in the decision-making process, students and parents want detailed information. Taking groups of low-income and first-generation college students on campus visits can be helpful. Information about college costs and financial aid are of special interest to parents. Low-income and first-generation college students and their parents can also benefit from mentoring programs to help them fill out college applications and student financial aid forms.

Finally, money matters. The educational aspirations of students, and the attitudes of parents, are influenced by college costs and financial aid. Efforts to maintain or expand our federal and state financial aid programs should be supported.

Continuing Research

Like all studies, this one answers few questions definitively and raises at least as many others. The most interesting finding is the relative importance of parents in the college decision-making process. Until the twelfth grade, parental support seems to be the most important factor in the development of educational aspirations beyond high school. Then, rather quickly, in the twelfth grade and one year after high school graduation, some of the traditional status-attainment variables, like parental income and education and student grade point average, emerge to play important roles in students' ability to actualize their plans.

Additional research is needed on this critical period that starts in the twelfth grade and ends one year after high school graduation. If we can better understand the barriers that first-generation and low-income students encounter during this pivotal period, we may discover more effective interventions to reduce the gap between some students' educational aspirations and their subsequent achievement. Dodge (1997) conducted a two-year longitudinal study of the college decision-making process of high school students during their junior and senior years. Using both survey data and intensive interviews, he focused on low-income students who aspired to be the first in their families to go to college. His results demonstrate that parental support, academic success in high school, the courses taken, peers, student aspirations, and unpredictable barriers interact in a complex and mutually shaping fashion to influence whether or not the students actualized their goals. This study and the ethnographic work of McDonough (1997) are illustrative of the kind of research needed to understand what happens to students during this critical time period. More focused attention on students of color, on women, and on middle-class students is needed.

This study, however, also illustrates that college choice, even immediately after graduation, is not a simple yes-no decision. Our final interviews with our subsample demonstrate that many students eventually went to some type of postsecondary institution. These students represent an understudied population. Given the public policy debates over workforce development and the need for a skilled technical labor force, delayed-entry students merit more research. New national longitudinal data sets such as the begininning postsecondary student longitudinal study (BPS) and the baccalaureate and beyond longitudinal study (B&B) should enable researchers to concentrate on this population.

Another intriguing line of inquiry for researchers is the potential link between how students structure their college decisions and their subsequent satisfaction with, and persistence in, their college of choice. The survey part of our study ended before the students who attended a college immediately after high school had completed their first year of classes. Thus, we lacked good measures of persistence. Nevertheless, some findings from this study and previous work (Braxton, Vesper, and Hossler, 1995; Hamrick and Hossler, 1995; and St. John, 1991) point to the possibility of relationships between the college-choice process and student persistence. Again, the longitudinal data sets (such as NELS) would help in examining this issue. From a sociological perspective, further work in this area will also extend our understanding the status-attainment process. At one level of analysis, this is the fundamental topic being examined throughout our study.

Finally, we recommend additional research into the role of external sources of information on the college-choice process. External sources of information appear to enable students to actualize their college plans. In addition, external information allows students to evaluate institutions in their consideration sets and to determine which school to attend. Several studies have looked at the effect on the college-choice process of college marketing materials (Anderson, 1994; Brodigan, 1985; Esteban and Appel, 1992; Litten and Hall, 1989) and of college guidebooks (Hossler and Foley, 1995; McDonough, 1997). However, little attempt has been made to look at how students learn about the characteristics of colleges and how they find out about specific colleges. We suggest that college marketing materials, college guidebooks, high school teachers and counselors, and college admissions counselors be considered external sources of information, thus providing us with a unifying construct for a systematic inquiry into their influence upon the final stages of the college-choice process. When linked with theories of information processing (Huber, 1984; Stinchcombe, 1990), an examination of the impact of external sources of information on students' college choice may provide theoretical and practical insights into this later stage of this complex phenomenon.

EACH FALL, APPROXIMATELY 62 percent of all high school graduates attend orientation sessions at the college of their choice (*Digest of Educational Statistics*, 1996). To outside observers this could appear to be a seamless, easy transition, and for some students, it is. For Sam, the only difficult decision was whether to attend Wabash College in Indiana or Eckerd College in Florida. And Todd's path after high school also appeared easy. But Sam and Todd are the exceptions. The experiences of Seth, Laura, and Allison are more typical. Seth was on track to graduate from Purdue University, but he attended two institutions to fulfill his aspirations. Laura eventually completed a certification program in dental hygiene, but her path was anything but smooth. Allison held several jobs after graduating from high school and talked wistfully about the need for more education. For most young adults, the first noncompulsory educational decision they make is anything but easy.

One of the authors later ran into Jerome in a large shopping mall in Bloomington, Indiana. Jerome was home for the graduation ceremony of his older brother, who had just completed his master's degree at Indiana University. Jerome was tending bar in Albuquerque. He offered the following observation: "It is really hard sometimes to figure out what you want to do when you are young. I think all I really knew when you first started talking to me is that I liked people. It may sound funny, but I really like bartending. I get to talk to a lot of interesting people. I am good at it. And I make good money. I may finish my degree some day—but I might not, too. I just don't know."

Appendix

Theories, Models, and Methodological Issues

COLLEGE CHOICE MODELS

Unlike other phenomena associated with the college experience (such as student attrition), research on student college choice has employed diverse methods, assumptions, and theoretical perspectives, frequently at the same time. On the other hand, much of the research conducted at individual institutions has been atheoretical, grounded in the practical problems of colleges and universities, and not readily transferable to other institutions. However, it is possible to bring some order to the research conducted on college choice.

We examine the theoretical frameworks and models used to study college choice in a chronology that parallels their development and use, an organization that provides insight into how research on college choice has developed and changed over time. By presenting theories and models in this fashion, we hope to demonstrate that the results from our longitudinal study draw upon both the individual theories and the details and insights of previous research.

We outline below three strands of theoretically based approaches, or models, for looking at the college decision-making process: (1)economic models, which are rooted in econometric assumptions that prospective college students are rational actors and make careful cost-benefit analyses, (2) status-attainment models, which are rooted in sociology, and (3) information-processing models, which share the rational assumptions posited in economic models but also incorporate information seeking. In recent years, four major models have been used to study college choice. These are essentially a combination of ideas from the theoretical perspectives of economics and sociology and are based on the work of Jackson (1982), Chapman (1984), Hanson and Litten (1982), and Hossler and Gallagher (1987). After considering these combined models, we introduce a perspective based on college choice as an information-gathering, information-processing, and decision-making activity.

We look at the process of college choice from the student's viewpoint and not from that of the college. Marketing research reveals that students often intuitively seek a match between their own personal characteristics and those of students already enrolled at a college (Zemsky and Oedel, 1983). From the viewpoint of colleges, the college-choice process begins with a large pool of prospective students that narrows down to those who actually enroll (Hanson and Litten, 1982). College choice in this case means identification and recruitment. Although it is certainly true that colleges select students, we are convinced that understanding college choice from the student's perspective can inform marketing approaches and help those charged with recruiting students.

As Litten (1982) has observed and as our own work has shown, college choice is a complex process. Moreover, most high school students go through it only once. Hence, our understanding of it must draw on many perspectives and can probably never be developed into a comprehensive theory of student college choice.

Economic Models

Economic, or more properly econometric, models of college choice are based on the idea that a student maximizes a utility (such as low cost and high quality), most often using cost-benefit analysis. Students must decide, for example, if they want to go to college, go into the workforce after high school, or join a military service. If the choice is made to continue schooling, the student must decide what kind of college to attend (vocational, community college, four-year institution) by weighing the costs against the perceived benefits. Once a type of school is chosen, the student must select from among a range of possible institutions. In a sense, economic models assume that a student's future is unlimited and filled with possible choices, which can be eliminated according to some clear criteria.

The costs of college choice include both direct and indirect expenses (tuition, books, opportunity costs), but they might also include losses incurred simply by leaving home, such as loss of friendships. Benefits could include the financial rewards derived from a degree from a particular institution, a location close to home, quality of student life, and extracurricular programs. Economic models assume that, as students consider colleges, they can detail the advantages and disadvantages of each, associate a utility or a value with the attributes of each, make reasonable assumptions about the outcomes of one decision over another, and then choose more or less rationally in order to maximize benefits and reduce costs (Hossler, Braxton, and Coopersmith, 1989).

Kotler and Fox (1985) have proposed a four-stage model of college choice based on risk reduction. It is a discrete process of evaluation and decision making that resembles a tree diagram: (1) make the initial decision to investigate colleges, (2) gather information in an orderly and comprehensive way, (3) evaluate and eliminate choices to generate a set of educational options, and (4) choose from among the options. Students weigh the costs and risks involved in each stage of the process. Costs and risks that are difficult to assign a dollar value to, such as parental expectations and encouragement, are assumed to be most influential to students during the first two stages (Young and Reyes, 1987). As a rule, these early stages evolve over longer time periods, and the variables that influence the outcomes are less precise and therefore more difficult for econometric models to deal with.

The Kotler and Fox model is typical of the economic models of college choice. By definition, economics is concerned with the study of the production and distribution of all scarce resources that individuals desire, such as income, wealth, and commodities (Cohn, 1979). Moreover, economists often study the allocation of resources among competing uses by designing strategies to assign values to those uses and ranking the resulting utilities. In most cases, economists assume that everything is known about the resources and their uses and that it is possible to assign a measurable value to the possibilities. It is also assumed that individuals will behave rationally—that is, in their best interest—and choose a resource that maximizes a utility. Thus a student with a high grade point average, high SAT scores, and high family monetary support or financial aid will choose a college of high selectivity at the least cost.

Despite the apparent complexity of some combined models, they use variants of a simple function basic to economics: the production and cost function. This function is designed so that outputs are clearly tied to inputs and the relationships are linear; that is, outputs are sums of inputs with appropriate weights. The inputs considered in many models of college choice are those usually associated with education: student characteristics (e.g., ability), family characteristics (e.g., income), school-related factors (e.g., class size), and perhaps even community-related factors (e.g., per capita income). The outputs, in this case, are college-choice decisions.

Even though many variables used in economic models are sociologically based, they are also typically associated with parental income, academic ability (Radner and Miller, 1970), and parents' educational level (Kohn, Manski, and Mundel, 1976; Bishop, 1977). Economic models focus on how individuals with certain characteristics (e.g., parental socioeconomic status, student gender, and student ability) differ in terms of the variables that are important when they choose a college. The emphasis is on the process of decision making and the ways in which different students rate and use different college attributes in making decisions. The presumption is that students have (near) perfect information and act rationally to maximize utilities. Unfortunately, students and their families do not always behave as rationally as economists assume. It might be that they lack perfect knowledge of their choices or that economics alone is insufficient to understand college choice.

Status-Attainment Models

Status-attainment models describe how variables interact as students make decisions about going to college or about which college to attend. If economic models open possibilities for students through rational choice, status-attainment models describe a process that has acted to narrow students' possibilities since they were born. From this perspective, different variables interact at different points during students' lives and during their college-choice decision-making process, and the influence of these variables may change over time.

Status-attainment models focus on how socialization processes, family conditions, interactions with peers, and school environments help shape students' college choices. These models assume that behavioral variables, such as students' academic performance or how their families spend their leisure time, interact with background variables, like the occupational status of parents, to determine students' educational aspirations (Sewell and Shah, 1978). Indeed, Sewell, Haller, and Portes (1969) went further, arguing that socioeconomic status, associated with the family and with mental ability as derived from the parents, is linked to educational attainment through the interaction of intermediate variables such as academic performance, the influences of significant others, and students' educational aspirations.

Most of the research in this area concentrates on the effects of socioeconomic status (i.e., fixed family background characteristics) in decisions about careers that lead to status attainment (Sewell and Shah, 1969; Sewell, Haller, and Portes, 1969). These studies consider (only weakly) the ways in which personal and family characteristics interact with the social and academic environment of high school to affect student decisions about educational aspirations (Boyle, 1966; Alwin and Otto, 1977). In these approaches, the variable of educational aspirations and its antecedents are of interest to us.

Besides the assumption of rationality used in economics, the status-attainment perspective differs from the econometric perspective in that it involves a more interactive process between variables that measure broad social constructs and variables that measure individual student characteristics. Models that combine both processes may have more explanatory power than single perspectives (Hossler, Braxton, and Coopersmith, 1989). Indeed, a major advantage of the combined models is that the researcher can choose variables

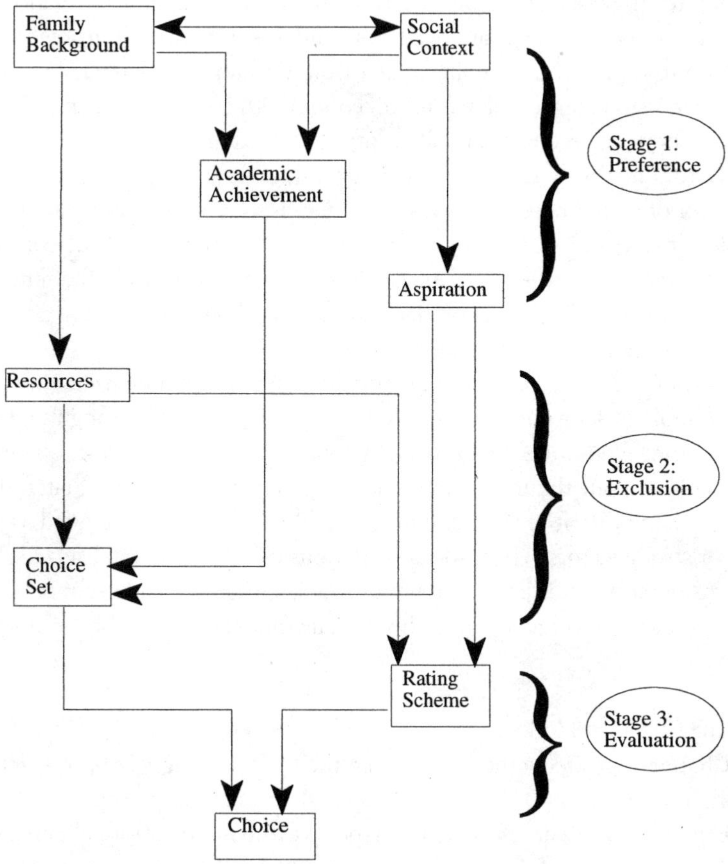

FIGURE A.1 The Jackson Combined Model (adapted from Jackson, 1982)

from either domain and concentrate on the sociological aspect of college choice as a process while maintaining the decision-making perspective of economics.

Combined Models

The four major combined models of college choice are from Jackson (1982), Chapman (1984), Hanson and Litten (1982), and Hossler and Gallagher (1987). Each is examined below.

The Jackson Model

Jackson's combined model has three stages: preference, exclusion, and evaluation (see figure A.1). In the preference stage, Jackson used sociological research to show that academic achievement has the strongest correlation with students' educational aspirations. Thus, students who do well in high school will tend to aspire to go to college, that is, to develop a preference for college. In the exclusion stage, Jackson used economic theory to assert that decision making about college is essentially a process of excluding institutions. Exclusion factors might be location or cost or academic quality. Jackson departed from economic theory by observing that decisions are not always rational and are often made on incomplete or inaccurate information. Once the consideration set is narrowed, the student evaluates the characteristics of the remaining colleges to make a final decision. Jackson has not, however, explained how the initial institutional sets are formed.

Jackson rated the variables influencing each stage. Family background and high school academic achievement were rated moderate to strong in all three stages. From economics, he drew on factors such as location, cost, quantity of information about the institution, and the job prospects of graduates. These factors are important in the last two stages of the model and are rated as moderate or strong factors. Thus, social conditions can define initial lists of schools for consideration and determine how variables interact, while economic variables can be used to exclude and choose. The model is reasonably grounded in theory.

The Chapman Model

Chapman posited a model in which the first two stages are presearch and search, followed by applications, choice, and enrollment (see figure A.2). This model involves both an individual perspective and an institutional perspective and suggests that the following student characteristics and external influences interact to form a student's general expectation of college life:

Student Characteristics

- ➡ Socioeconomic status
- ➡ Scholastic aptitude
- ➡ Educational aspirations
- ➡ Academic performance

External Influences

- ➡ Significant others (friends, parents, high school personnel
- ➡ College characteristics (cost, location, programs)
- ➡ College marketing efforts (written information, campus visits, recruiting

In the presearch stage, family income has a direct effect on which colleges are considered. Moreover, students tend to select colleges that enroll students with academic ability similar to their own. These variables may limit these ini-

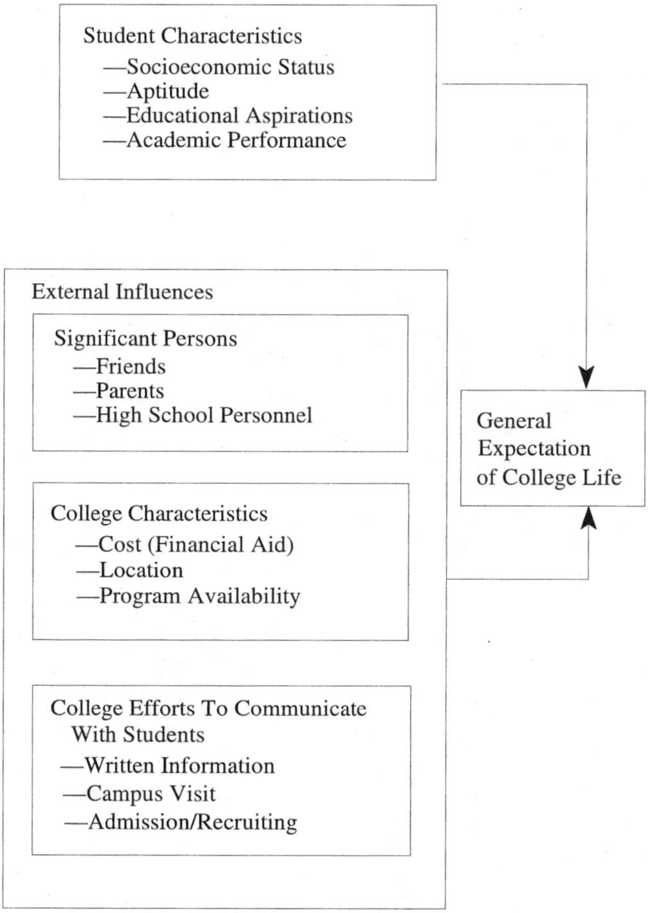

FIGURE A.2 The Chapman Model (adapted from Chapman, 1984)

tial choices. In the search stage, students gather information about particular institutions. However, they are essentially on a fishing expedition, because they do not know what questions to ask. The later stages are straightforward, especially the application and enrollment stages. Most of the work in the college decision-making process is done in the search stage.

The Hanson and Litten Model

One of Hanson and Litten's major contributions to college choice was their description of it as a continuing process, proposing a five-step process: having college aspirations; starting the search process; gathering information; sending applications; and enrolling (see figure A.3). These five steps can be combined into three stages: one, the decision to participate in postsecondary education;

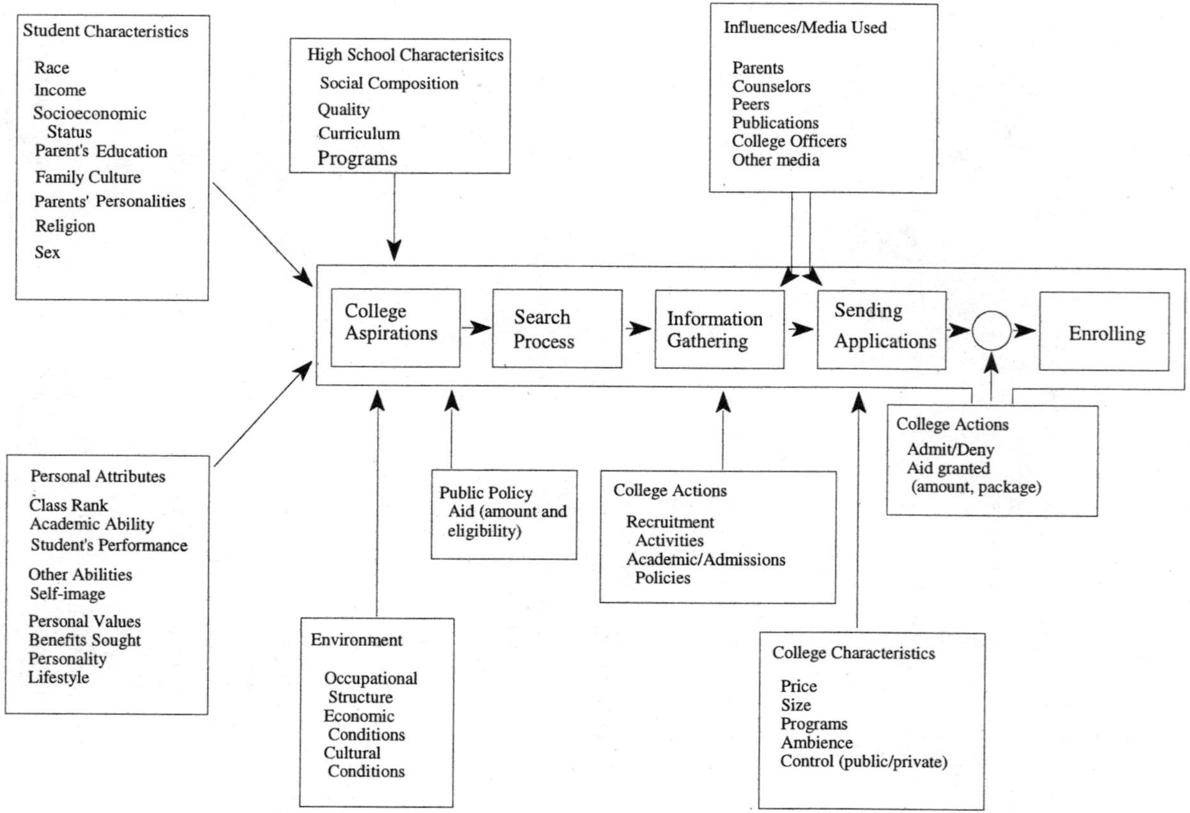

FIGURE A.3 The Hanson and Litten Model (adapted from Hanson and Litten, 1982)

FIGURE A.4 The Hossler and Gallagher Model (adapted from Hossler and Gallagher, 1987)

two, the investigation of institutions and the development of sets of institutions to consider; and three, the process of applying and enrolling.

Hanson and Litten identified broad sets of variables that affect the college-choice process: background characteristics, such as parental income and education, race, gender; personal characteristics, such as academic ability, class rank, self-image; high school characteristics, such as social compostition, programs, and curriculum; and colleges characteristics, such as cost, size, programs, and timeliness in responding to student inquiries. They also introduce public policy (e.g., financial aid policy) as a determining influence. Hanson and Litten's approach can be viewed as a cross between Jackson's student-based model and the more institution-based Chapman model. For example, studies have shown that higher levels of parental education are associated with student preference for private colleges and that parental encouragement is positively associated with students' decisions to attend more selective institutions (Litten, Sullivan, and Brodigan, 1983).

The Hossler and Gallagher Model

Hossler and Gallagher have proposed a simpler yet more conceptual model of college choice (figure A.4). Based partially on a synthesis and simplification of previous work, the Hossler and Gallagher model isolates and contains the process within a manageable framework of three stages, which emphasize the student rather than the institution: *predisposition*, or the decision to go to college instead of taking alternative status-attainment paths, such as work or military service; *search*, or the process of learning about specific institutions and their characteristics; and *choice*, the stage when applications are completed and the student chooses a particular institution.

The predisposition stage is akin to the notion of educational aspiration, but it differs in that the emphasis is not on the intention but rather on the decision to do something, that is, to go to college. The search stage is the period when students seek information about college opportunities. There is increased interaction between students and institutions during this stage. Drawing upon Chapman's observations, Hossler and Gallagher assumed that the search process consists of searching both for institutional attributes and for institutions to consider. To them, this stage is the most important one and the one most amenable to intervention. While in the critical process of searching, the student is in effect making lists of both college attributes and colleges. The Hossler and Gallagher model assumes that these lists will be tempered by students' social conditions and influenced in nontrivial ways by what students learn about colleges. That is, not only will students' change which colleges are on their lists, they will also learn new questions to ask and new ways to conduct their searches.

The choice stage assumes that students have made application decisions consistent with the search stage: they apply to schools they have previously selected and in a preference order consistent with, but not necessarily the same as, the selection order. For example, if students select three colleges during the search stage, they might apply to only two and might prefer only one of these. During the choice stage, students compare the academic and social attributes of each college they have applied to and seek the best value with the greatest benefits.

The model is primarily sociological. Background characteristics are correlated with the predisposition stage, the point at which students choose to go to college. These background characteristics are cumulative in terms of their effect upon the college-choice process, varying only in their level of influence during the several stages of the process; they always operate.

The Information-Processing Model

In the discussion so far, most of the models have used information gathering as part of the college-choice process, but information gathering is not the same as information processing. To process information means to make decisions as to what issues require decisions as well as using information to make exclusion or evaluation statements about the issues that require decisions. It is a continuous process of reducing uncertainty—for our purposes, uncertainty about what college characteristics to consider and then about which college to attend. To gather information, process it, and make decisions is cyclical (figure A.5). Uncertainty at each stage is reduced, and the outputs of one stage become the inputs of the next (Stinchcombe, 1990). The unit of analysis is the student in a social setting seeking and using information to make informed decisions about colleges.

There are no coherent theories of information processing in the same sense that there are economic theories or sociological theories, although Stinchcombe and others (Huber, 1984) have moved in that direction. (Our approach to information processing should not be confused with information theory as used by computer scientists or electrical engineers; these researchers do not use sociology, and we use very little mathematics.) Information processing is a perspective (or lens) that makes gathering and processing information in a social

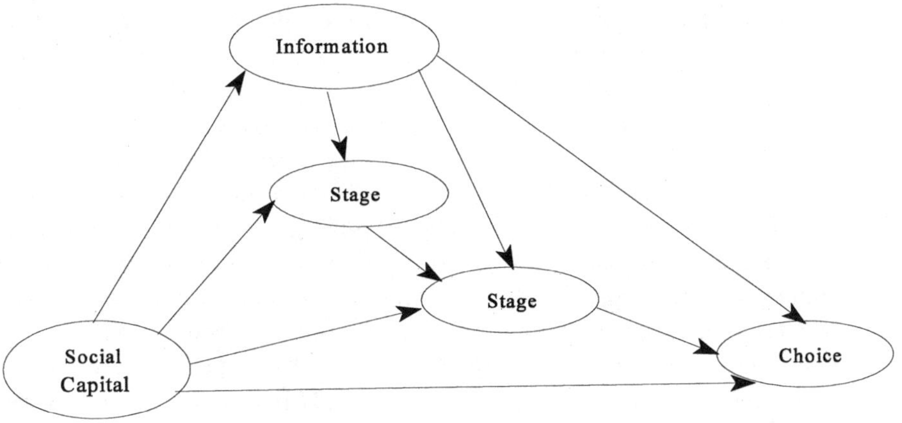

FIGURE A.5 The Information-Processing Model

setting an essential part of decision making rather than a prerequisite to it. Taking this perspective means we must consider aspects of decision-making theory and sociology, especially social capital and socialization. Information processing, social capital, and cultural capital together allow us to introduce into the college-choice process dynamic roles for parents, peers, and schools. We use sociology, decision making, and information processing to present additional ways to understand college choice. Information processing might help us understand the least explored part of the college-choice process, the search stage. Cultural capital, particularly Bourdieu's (1977) concept of habitus, is a useful lens for looking at some aspects of students' final matriculation decisions.

Social Capital, Cultural Capital, and Socialization

Sociological theory can be used to enhance our understanding of the college-choice process. First, sociological variables such as student background characteristics (e.g., ability as measured by grade point average) and family factors (e.g., parents' education and income) are the foundation of much of the work on status attainment and the college-choice process (Sewell and Hauser, 1975; Hearn, 1984; Stage and Hossler, 1989; Hossler and Vesper, 1990; Hossler, Vesper, and Braxton, 1991). Coleman (1987, 1990) has described social capital as a complex set of factors and relationships that exists in a close-knit group such as a family. Social capital forms the basis for the way in which parents help to define the future of their children. The time parents invest in raising their children, the energy they use, and the support they give them, especially the support and encouragement to go to college, are key ingredients of social capital as applied to education. Other educational aspects of social capital are parents of modest education who through example impart a love of reading or a belief in the importance of education in their children. Families and friends who encourage critical thinking also increase a child's social capital.

Cultural capital as developed by Bourdieu (1977) and McDonough (1997) share some properties with social capital. McDonough has described cultural capital as shared preferences and attitudes that upper-class and middle-class families transmit to their children. These preferences and attitudes provide a mechanism for maintaining class status and privileges. Preference for a college education and advanced degrees is one form of cultural capital that enables middle-class and upper middle-class families to retain their economic status. Like economic capital, cultural capital is invested to secure resources and achieve goals. McDonough has used Bourdieu's concept of habitus to examine the college destinations of high school students. Habitus is an internalized set of experiences, outlooks, and beliefs that individuals accumulate from their immediate environment. McDonough has attached particular importance to high schools and their influence upon matriculation decisions. High school teachers, counselors, and peers help to develop a belief in college as an acceptable destination.

Social capital is useful in understanding college choice for three reasons. First, social capital provides the currency students can use to make decisions about going to college (and being successful, once enrolled) (Coleman, 1987). Second, social capital is available outside of the home, whereas socioeconomic status is not; thus, students' futures might not be based only on the status of their parents. Third, social capital provides a mechanism for the interaction of students and their families that goes beyond the discrete effects usually considered as determinants in the educational aspiration literature. Family and students change each other's behavior, support each other, and act as a unit to accomplish a task—in this case, to search for and choose a college.

Students' three main socializing agents are the family, the peer group, and the school. The first two are primary and are both personalized and informal. But the value they place on education, including expectations and support, has an important impact on students' movement through the education system. In particular, family and friends have an impact on students' predisposition to go to college, their search strategies, and their college choices. The socialization effects of schools most noticeably come through teachers and those charged with aiding students to negotiate the high school experience, such as counselors (Hearn, 1984; McDonough, 1997). The school affects student socialization by such support for students as offering college preparatory and vocational curriculum tracks; in addition, teachers' encouragement and counselors' attitudes are important.

The interaction among students, family, and school is an extension of the process of socialization by which children acquire the values, concepts, and behavioral norms that shape their actions as adults (DiMaggio, 1982; Clark, 1983; Epstein and Karweit, 1983). But within the frameworks of social capital and cultural capital, socialization does not have discrete and one-time effects, as appears so often to be the case in the sociology of status attainment. Rather, for many students it operates through a substantial length of time, particularly while they are in high school.

Information Processing

Our information-based approach to college choice puts the emphasis on the student as an information-gathering and information-processing agent. Information about colleges gained by a student in the ninth grade might determine the characteristics of colleges the student considers in the tenth grade. Information gathered in the tenth grade might determine that in the eleventh grade a student will consider only public colleges (or only colleges with a reputation in science, or only those with a strong athletic program). As time goes by, uncertainty is reduced.

An information-processing perspective has a sociological bent, which is lacking in economic models (Stinchcombe, 1990). Students' information gathering and information processing is a social activity and is embedded in, and perhaps limited by, interactions with family, friends, and school. To understand college choice, we must therefore consider the sociology and the rationality of economics and decision making. Indeed, information processing is best understood in a social context and thus draws upon both sociological and economic constructs.

Although similarities exist between information processing and decision making, there are essential differences. Classic decision making is one of a number of steps used in the information-processing model, but it is by no means the model itself. In a classic decision-making model (Trueman, 1977), all possible choices can be determined from the information gathered in order to attach the appropriate level of importance to each alternative. The classic decision-making process is similar to turning a crank on a machine that sums the various weighted options and selects the most efficient. Through the ability to lay out all alternatives, students are assumed (1) to know the possible outcomes of their choices, (2) to know what information they need to rank their alternatives, and (3) to know how to deliberate about these alternatives. In short, students going through a process for the first, and possibly only, time must have the experience and knowledge of seasoned observers of college choice in order to effectively apply decision-making theory.

There is a second major distinction between decision making and information processing. In its strictest form, one of the guiding assumptions of economic decision making is that two people with the same background who are given the same information and with the same outcomes in mind will make the same decisions essentially in the same way (Trueman, 1977). But a guiding assumption of information processing is that, even if there is the same information and the same desired outcomes, the same decisions will often not be made; or if they are, the reasons for doing so can be very different (Stinchcombe, 1990). One reason for this is that, as information processing progresses, different social groups (e.g., the student and family) use their social capital differently in the process of reducing uncertainty.

For example, two children from the same family who have gone to the same high school, with similar achievement levels and financial constraints, might choose to go to two different kinds of college, one public the other private. One of the students might borrow money to go to the private college, while the other might prefer full parental financial support at the public college. Both students start in the same place but end up in different places. Contrast this with two other students, one from a well-to-do and well-educated family who talks to her parents, who has been taught to be independent, and who gathers information to convince her parents that a public college is her best choice. But a young man from a similarly situated family might accept his father's insistence that his alma mater, a public school, is a better choice than a private school. Both students start with similar backgrounds in terms of classical sociology and both end up considering public institutions, but they get to that point in different ways.

In classic decision making, the gathering and deciding functions are often separated. The individual who gathers the information typically does so at the behest of another individual, who is the decision maker. Classic decision making assumes that gatherers are not capable of deciding but that deciders know what must be gathered. This model is often followed, for example, in institutional research. In this context, students would know what they need to find out and would find people to gather information for them (such as parents or counselors). Once the information was gathered, students would rationally choose from among the options laid out for them. However, even in an information-gathering and information-processing model, in which the family and student gather information, process it, and make college-choice decisions, there are two ways in which information might be gathered: internally and externally. Some families, because of extensive previous experience with higher education, might be able to gather information and make decisions internally, with little or no external assistance. On the other hand, parents who have not attended college might not be able to gather information without assistance and might have to rely on external sources. This view of seeking information externally is consistent with Coleman's (1990) view that social capital originates in many places, not only the family.

The combined perspectives of social capital, socialization, decision making, and information processing offer important new perspectives on student college choice. When synthesized in an information-processing perspective, they provide fresh insights. Although the search stage of college choice might be difficult to develop into a comprehensive theory, information processing has promise in that direction. It may more closely parallel the later stages of the college-choice process than any college-choice model developed to date. Indeed, information-processing model complements the search and choice processes of college choice outlined by Chapman (1984) and Hossler and Gallagher (1987).

Figure A-5 shows the three components of an information-processing model: social capital and information acting, through stages, to determine where a student goes to college. The three components could correspond to tenth, eleventh, and twelfth grades. During the stages, students might engage in a a variety of activities that constitute search, and so different variables could be used at each stage to measure the search process. The model is discrete, because each stage is a separate search. Search is not a single variable; it is only by layering and connecting the information from several stages that an understanding of the college-choice process can be made. College choice is best understood as a process, which requires different variables at different times, as the student moves from predisposition, to search, to choice. The unifying theme is that the variables enable students to gather and process information while reducing uncertainty about which colleges to consider and apply to.

Summary

Decision-making models are based on economic theory, on sociology derived from status-attainment theory, and on an information-processing model that expands on decision-making and status-attainment theories. Each of the models have advantages and disadvantages in understanding college choice. Indeed, the variety of strategies indicates that research on college choice is not closed: college choice is a complex process. Most high school students go through the college-choice process only once and yet each college-bound student might repeat parts of the process (e.g., the search stage). Choosing a college is not a skill students intend to sharpen with a view to using again. Hence, understanding college choice is itself complicated.

It may be that, while status-attainment and social capital models are useful for understanding the formation of educational aspirations, information-processing theory is valuable for viewing how students search for colleges and how they gather and process information about colleges. Econometric theories combined with the cultural capital model may provide the most serviceable perspectives on how students formulate their final consideration sets and how they decide what college they will go to.

METHODOLOGY AND ANALYSIS

Below, we outline the sampling, instrumentation, and data analysis of our nine-year longitudinal study.

Sampling

The first two survey instruments and the sample of students and parents that formed the foundation for this study were part of a pilot study conducted by the Indiana Career and Postsecondary Advancement Center, or ICPAC.[1] In 1986–87, twenty-one high schools, with approximately 4,923 ninth-grade students (and their parents), were surveyed. The return rate for the ninth-grade survey was 63 percent.

Cluster sampling was used to select the twenty-one high schools to represent the ethnic, socioeconomic, and geographical diversity of Indiana residents (urban/rural, northern/southern) (Miller, 1991). Cluster sampling techniques result in some methodological problems: the sample is not random, and it may not be truly representative of the total population being studied. This can reduce independence among the characteristics being studied and increase the probabilities of Type I errors.

When the ninth-grade students in the sample entered their sophomore year, funding for a follow-up survey was once again provided by ICPAC. However, the amount of money available was less, and only students, not parents, were surveyed. The return rate was 29 percent.

In the spring of 1988, we received funding from the Lilly Endowment to continue our study for three more years. Students were surveyed twice during their junior and senior years, once in the fall and once in the spring, and were surveyed again in January following the year they graduated from high school. Parents received one survey during the junior year and one during the senior year. Despite the additional funding, we experienced response rate problems during the last three years of the study. Not surprisingly, students who were not planning to continue their education were less likely to complete their surveys.

---

1. A statewide, postsecondary encouragement program created in 1986 to work with high school students in Indiana. The center is under the direction of the Indiana Commission for Higher Education and communicates with approximately 275,000 Indiana households per year.

By the time students entered the spring of their senior year, budget constraints and response rates forced a change in our survey strategy. To enable us to invest resources into meaningful response rates, we sent surveys only to students who had responded to two of the previous three surveys. This strategy enabled us to send more reminders and a second copy of each survey to the students and parents most likely to return completed surveys. As a result, students planning to attend four-year colleges were overrepresented in the later years of our longitudinal study. Our findings may thus understate statistical significance, because the small numbers of respondents not planning to go to college reduced variation in the samples.

In addition to our surveys, a subsample of fifty-six students and their parents were individually interviewed nine times between 1989 and 1994. In the first year of our study, when students were enrolled in the ninth grade, no interviews were conducted. During their sophomore year (1987–88), with the assistance of high school guidance counselors, we conducted group interviews with students and parents (seven to ten students or parents were interviewed at once). Unfortunately, because we did not anticipate additional funding at that time, we did not keep the names of the participants on file. Therefore, when we later received long-term funding from the Lilly Endowment, we were not able to include the same students in the systematic individual interviews we conducted in subsequent years.

Students and parents for the interview subsample were selected from eight of the twenty-one high schools in the original sample. The selection criteria used to identify the eight high schools included residence (urban, suburban, rural), ethnicity (African American and Caucasian), and income (low, medium, and high). *T*-tests comparing the student background characteristics of this subsample to the total sample revealed no significant differences (Hossler and Stage, 1987). A small number of students and parents whom we interviewed frequently between 1989 and 1994 (junior year through one year after high school) were also interviewed during their sophomore year (1988–89). The number was very small—only four students (and their parents)—and they were all from one high school, because the high school counselor recalled which students she had invited to the sophomore group interview. Nevertheless, the themes evident from surveys completed by sophomores, and subsequent interviews and surveys completed in the junior year, revealed patterns that made us comfortable using insights gained from the group interviews conducted during the sophomore year.

Students from the eight high schools who completed the ninth-grade survey were placed on three lists. One list was for students who, in the ninth grade, planned to go to college (the going cohort). The second list was for those students who were undecided about their after-high-school plans (the undecided cohort). The third list was for those students who planned to work immediately after high school (the not-going cohort). Counselors were given the list of qualified students and asked to select three students from the going cohort, two students from the undecided cohort, and two from the not-going cohort. Fifty-six students and their parents were part of this qualitative study.

During the next six years, students were interviewed nine times: three times during their junior year, four times during their senior year, one time during the first year after high school graduation, and one time during the fourth year after high school graduation. Four interviews were conducted in person, five by telephone. Parents, usually only one, were interviewed four times (twice in 1988–89 and twice in 1989–90; they were not interviewed in 1991 or 1994). Unless parents failed to attend scheduled interviews, all parent interviews were conducted in person.

All students were first-year students in high school when the study began and had been out of high school for four years when the study concluded. By 1994 some students were seniors, others had been in and out of more than one college, others had permanently dropped out, while others were planning to enroll for the first time. Some students were working, others had joined the military service, and some had gotten married.

Instrumentation

The first surveys used for ninth-grade students and parents were developed and extensively field tested for readability, content, and face validity. Items were derived from previous research in the areas of adolescent development, status attainment, and college-choice research. After the first year, an iterative and interactive approach was used to devise survey items. Although we continued to explore questions raised from previous adolescent development, status attainment, and college-choice research, we also included survey items that would enable us to explore themes emerging from the analysis of our surveys and interviews. For example, we had not originally planned to focus on the effect of college costs, financial aid, or information. We believe this is one of the strengths of our research design: we were able to use emergent designs typically associated with qualitative research designs, in a longitudinal study that combined the advantages of survey and qualitative methods.

The interview questions were open-ended. Like our surveys, they were developed by drawing on theories of adolescent development and models of student college choice as well as ongoing data analysis of interview and survey results. All interviews were recorded; later, summary transcripts were prepared. These tapes, transcripts, and associated field notes became the primary data source for this study.

Data Analysis

Our data included the results from both surveys and interviews. Thus, we used statistical and qualitative analytical methods. In our analyses of survey data, we used a variety of statistical approaches. In some cases, simple descriptive statistics were the most appropriate and useful way to summarize characteristics of respondents, the types of institution they were considering, or what they did after they graduated from high school.

In several instances, we used multivariate analytical techniques. For example, to determine how consistent students were with respect to the types of college they were considering in tenth, eleventh, and twelfth grades, we used discriminant analysis, because the criterion variable was dichotomous (Hossler and Vesper, 1993). For each institutional characteristic (selectivity, cost, in state or out of state), students were judged either to be consistent or not consistent over time (they were assigned a value of 1 if they were consistent and 0 if they were not consistent).

Factor analysis was frequently used as a data-reduction technique. Because of the large number of variables, we often used exploratory factor analysis to reduce the number of variables. As noted, we included multiple measures of constructs of interest to increase the reliability of our measures. Thus, several questions probed students' and parents' desire for more information about financial aid, and several probed their knowledge of types of financial aid (Hossler and Maple, 1993). Using factor analysis, we discovered that these questions typically clustered in one factor, which could be used when we used other statistical techniques, like linear multiple regression and path modeling (Lisrel).

Schmit (1991) created a temporal model of college search activities, using Lisrel to examine the effects of endogenous and exogenous variables over time. Hossler and Stage (1992) used Lisrel to create a structural model of the factors that influence the development of educational aspirations. We also examined factors that were predictive of parents' college savings. In this instance, logistic regression was used. Because the variables we were looking at included both dichotomous and interval variables and because we assumed that the relationships among the variables were linear, logistic linear regression was the best choice.

In other instances we used less sophisticated statistical techniques, such as frequency distributions. In a study of the college characteristics most important to students in our sample as they began to decide which college to attend, we used ANOVA as one analytical method (Hossler, Vesper, and Braxton, 1991). In this case, we wanted to see if the extent to which discrete student background characteristics like grade point average, gender, and educational aspirations might differentially be correlated with institutional characteristics.

Qualitative data reduction and analytic techniques were used for several studies. For example, Bouse and Hossler (1991) used both quantitative and qualitative analytic techniques to examine students' and parents' knowledge of college costs and financial aid. An entire interview of students and parents in the subsample was devoted to knowledge of college costs and student financial aid. Using data reduction and coding techniques described by Miles and Huberman (1984), categories of knowledge were developed and then used to create scales for each student and parent. These were subsequently analyzed using chi-square tests of significance, ANOVAs, and linear multiple regression statistical techniques. In another study, Schmit and Hossler (1995) used analytical methods derived from by Glaser and Strauss (1967) and Lincoln and Guba (1985) to uncover major themes that influenced the college decisions of the fifty-six students during the years after they graduated from high school. First, major themes were identified and more formal categories were developed for data analysis and interpretation. When using qualitative analytic techniques, the researchers would meet regularly as we proceeded through the first round of data analysis, discussing emerging themes, developing a common coding format for the data, and triangulating data to ensure that we were using similar approaches to search and code the interview data.

Design Limitations

The longitudinal nature of this study, the inclusion of parents, and the iterative development of surveys and interview protocol make this study unique. However, it is not without significant flaws. Drawing the sample solely from the state of Indiana limited the representativeness of the sample. Family income and educational levels in Indiana rank in the bottom quartile of the fifty states. Since family education is directly correlated with college aspirations and participation, the generally lower incomes of Indiana families are likely to have had subtle influences on our results. Had our sample included more students from higher-income families, we may have had more students who thought about college at an earlier age. More students might also have considered attending out-of-state, private, or highly selective colleges.

In addition, Indiana is not as ethnically diverse as the nearby states of Illinois, Michigan, and Ohio. African Americans generally start their college search process later and are less likely to attend costly and selective private colleges. They are also less likely to rely on parents and more likely to seek guidance from ministers, teachers, and other members of the community as they consider their post–high school options. Latino students are more likely to attend a college close to home and to rely on their parents and other family members as they make their educational decisions (Hossler, Braxton, and Coopersmith, 1989; Paulsen, 1990).

Finally, Indiana does not have a large state college system or many highly regarded national universities. The composition of Indiana's college system directly affects educational opportunities within the state and, therefore, affects the search and choice stages of the college-choice process.

SUMMARY

Because of the longitudinal nature of our study, there was constant interplay between the theoretical and empirical leads provided by previous studies of adolescent development, status attainment, and college choice and the findings gleaned from our own work. Our own analyses often led to new insights, which caused us to go back to the research literature, to conduct additional analyses of our own data, and to add new questions to the next survey or interview. This constant interaction of theory, analysis, and data gathering occurred throughout our work. It was an enriching experience and greatly enhanced our work.

References

Abrahamson, T., and Hossler, D. 1990. Applying marketing strategies in student recruitment. In D. Hossler and J. Bean, eds., *The Strategic Management of College Enrollments*. San Francisco: Jossey-Bass.

Alexander, K., D'Amico, R., Fennessey, J., and McDill, E. 1978. *Status Composition and Educational Goals: An Attempt at Clarification*. Washington, D.C.: National Institute of Education.

Alwin, D., and Otto, L. 1977. Higher school context effects on aspirations. *Sociology of Education* 50:259–73.

Anderson, C. 1994. "Dear prospective student": An analysis of admissions material from four universities. *College and University* 70:27–38.

Anderson, M., and Hearn, J. 1992. Equity issues in higher education outcomes. In W. Becker and D. Lewis, eds., *The Economics of American Higher Education*. Boston: Kluwer.

Bateman, J. 1990. Correlates of black and white student predisposition to pursue postsecondary education. Ph.D. diss., Indiana University.

Becker, G. 1964. *Human Capital: A Theoretical and Empirical Analysis with Special Reference to Education*. New York: National Bureau of Economic Research.

Bishop, J. 1977. The effect of public policies on the demand for higher education. *Journal of Human Resources* 5:285–307.

Bourdieu, P. 1977. Cultural reproduction and social reproduction. In J. Karabel and A. Halsey, eds., *Power and Ideology in Education*. New York: Oxford University Press.

Bouse, G., and Hossler, D. 1991. A longitudinal study of student college choice: A progress report. *Journal of College Admissions* (winter): 11–16.

Bowen, H. 1977. *Investment in Learning: Individual and Social Value of American Education*. San Francisco: Jossey-Bass.

Boyer, E. 1987. *College: The Undergraduate Experience in America*. New York: Harper and Row.

Boyle, R. 1966. The effect of high school on student aspirations. *American Journal of Sociology* 71:628–39.

Braxton, J., Vesper, N., and Hossler, D. 1995. Incorporating college choice constructs into Tinto's model of student departure: Fulfillment of expectations for institutional traits and student withdrawal plans. *Research in Higher Education* 36:595–612.

Brodigan, D. 1985. Perceptions of college price and quality. *Journal of Higher Education Management* (summer/fall): 19–32.

Brown, K. 1982. Postsecondary plans of high school seniors in 1972 and 1980: Implications for student quality. Paper presented at AIR Forum, Denver.

Carpenter, P., and Fleishman, J. 1987. Linking intentions and behavior: Australian students' college plans and college attendance. *American Educational Research Journal* 24:79–105.

Chapman, D. 1981. A model of student college choice. *Journal of Higher Education* 52:490–505.

Chapman, R. 1984. *Toward a Theory of College Choice: A Model of College Search and Choice Behavior*. Alberta, Canada: University of Alberta Press.

Chapman, R., and Jackson, R. 1987. *College Choices of Academically Able Students: The Influence of No-Need Financial Aid and Other Factors*. New York: College Board.

Clark, C. 1993. The relationship between student characteristics and the postsecondary educational institutions considered during the search stage of the college choice process. Ph.D. diss., Indiana University.

Clark, R. 1983. *Family Life and School Achievement: Why Poor Black Children Succeed and Fail.* Chicago: University of Chicago Press.

Cohn, E. 1979. The costs of formal education in the United States, 1950–1975. *Journal of Education Finance* 3:70–81.

Coleman, J. 1966. Peer culture and education in modern society. In T. Newcomb and E. Wilson, eds., *College Peer Groups: Problems and Prospects for Research*. Chicago: Aldine.

———. 1987. *Public and Private High Schools: The Impact of Communities*. New York: Basic Books.

———. 1990. *Foundations of Social Theory*. Cambridge: Harvard University Press.

College Board. 1996. *Update: Trends in Student Aid, 1990–1996*. New York: College Board.

Conklin, M., and Dailey, A. 1981. Does consistency of parental encouragement matter for secondary students? *Sociology of Education* 54:254–62.

DeYoung, A. 1989. *Economics and American Education: A Historical and Critical Overview of the Impact of Economic Theories on Schooling in the United States.* New York: Longman.

Digest of Educational Statistics. 1996. Washington, D.C: National Center for Educational Statistics.

DiMaggio, P. 1982. Cultural capital and school success: The impact of status culture participation on the grades of U.S. high school students. *American Sociological Review* 47:189–201.

Dodge, R. 1997. The Twenty-first Century Scholars Program: Beyond high hopes and long odds. Ph.D. diss., Indiana University.

Epstein, J., and Karweit, N. 1983. *Friends in School: Patterns of Selection and Influence in Secondary Schools.* New York: Academic.

Esteban, J., and Appel, C. 1992. A student's eye view of direct mail marketing. *Journal of College Admissions* (spring): 21–28.

Falsey, B., and Haynes, B. 1984. The college channel: Private and public schools reconsidered. *Sociology of Education* 57:111–22.

Flint, T. 1993. Early awareness of college financial aid: Does it expand choice? *Review of Higher Education* 16:309–27.

Freeman, H. 1984. Impact of no-need scholarships on the matriculation decisions of academically talented students. Paper presented at the annual meeting of the American Association of Higher Education, Chicago.

Gallotti, K., and Mark, M. 1994. How do high school students structure an important life decision? A short-term longitudinal study of the college decision-making process. *Research in Higher Education* 35:589–607.

Glaser, B., and Strauss, A. 1967. *The Discovery of Grounded Theory*. Chicago: Aldine.

Hamrick, F., and Hossler, D. 1995. Active and passive searching in postsecondary educational decision making. *Review of Higher Education* 19:179–98.

Hanson, K., and Litten, L. 1982. Mapping the road to academia: A review of research on women, men, and the college selection process. In P. Perun, ed., *The Undergraduate Woman: Issues in Education*. Lexington, Mass.: Lexington.

Hearn, J. 1984. The relative roles of academic ascribed and socioeconomic characteristics in college destinations. *Sociology of Education* 57: 22–30.

Hossler, D., and Bean, J., eds. 1990. *The Strategic Management of College Enrollments*. San Francisco: Jossey-Bass.

Hossler, D., Braxton, J., and Coopersmith, G. 1989. Understanding student college choice. In J. Smart, ed., *Higher Education: Handbook of Theory and Research*. Vol. 4. New York: Agathon.

Hossler, D., and Foley, E. 1995. Reducing the noise in the college choice process: The use of college guidebooks and ratings. *New Directions for Institutional Research* 88:21–30.

Hossler, D., and Gallagher, K. 1987. Studying college choice: A three-phase model and the implication for policy makers. *College and University* 2:207–21.

Hossler, D., and Litten, L. 1993. *Mapping the Higher Education Landscape*. New York: College Board.

Hossler, D., and Maple, S. 1993. An investigation of the factors which differentiate among high school students planning to attend a postsecondary educational institution and those who are undecided. *Review of Higher Education* 16:285–307.

Hossler, D., and Stage, F. 1987. *An Analysis of Student and Parent Data from the Pilot Year of the Indiana College Placement and Assessment Center*. Bloomington: Indiana College Placement and Assessment Center.

———. 1992. Family and high school experience influences on the postsecondary plans of ninth-grade students: A structural model of predisposition to college. *American Educational Research Journal* 29:425–51.

Hossler, D., and Vesper, N. 1990. Effects of mother's education and employment upon the plans of high school students. Paper presented at the annual meeting of the American Educational Research Association, Boston.

———. 1993. Factors associated with parental college savings. *Journal of Higher Education* 64:140–66.

Hossler, D., Vesper, N., and Braxton, J. 1991. What really counts: An investigation of the factors associated with the perceived importance of college attributes among high school students. Paper presented at the annual meeting of the Association for the Study of Higher Education, Boston.

Huber, G. 1984. The nature and design of post-industrial organizations. *Management Science* 8:928–51.

Jackson, G. 1978. Financial aid and student enrollment. *Journal of Higher Education* 49:548–74.

———. 1982. Public efficiency and private choice in higher education. *Educational Evaluation and Policy Analysis* 4:237–47.

Jencks, C., et al. 1972. *Inequality: A Reassessment of the Effects of Family and Schooling in America*. New York: Basic Books.

Kerchoff, A., and Campbell, R. 1977. Race and status differences in the explanation of educational ambition. *Social Forces* 55:701–14.

Kohn, M., Manski, C., and Mundel, D. 1976. An empirical investigation of factors influencing college-going behaviors. *Annals of Economic and Social Measurement* 5:391–419.

Kotler, P., and Fox, K. 1985. *Strategic Marketing for Educational Institutions*. Englewoods Cliffs, N.J.: Prentice-Hall.

Leslie, L., and Brinkman, P. 1988. *The Economic Value of Higher Education*. New York: Macmillan.

Lewis, G., and Morrison, J. 1975. *A Longitudinal Study of College Selection*. Technical Report 2. Pittsburgh: School of Urban Public Affairs, Carnegie-Mellon University.

Lincoln, Y., and Guba, E. 1985. *Naturalistic Inquiry*. Beverly Hills, Calif.: Sage.

Litten, L. 1982. Different strokes in the applicant pool: Some refinements in a model of student college choice. *Journal of Higher Education* 53:383–402.

Litten, L., and Hall, A. 1989. In the eyes of the beholder: Some evidence on how high-school students and their parents view quality in colleges. *Journal of Higher Education* 60:303–24.

Litten, L., Sullivan, D., and Brodigan, P. 1983. *Applying Market Research in College Admissions*. New York: College Board.

Maguire, J., and Lay, R. 1981. Modeling the college choice process. *College and University* 56:123–39.

Manski, C., and Wise, D. 1983. *College Choice in America*. Cambridge: Harvard University Press.

McDonough, P. 1994. Buying and selling higher education: The social construction of the college applicant. *Journal of Higher Education* 65:427–46.

———. 1997. *Choosing Colleges: How Social Class and Schools Structure Opportunity*. Albany: State University of New York Press.

McGregor, E. 1994. *Economic Development and Public Education: Strategies and Standards*. Indianapolis: School of Public and Environment Affairs, Indiana University.

Michigan Higher Education Institute. 1993. *Beyond High School: Steps into the Future*. East Lansing: Michigan State University.

Miles, M., and Huberman, A. 1984. *Qualitative Data Analysis: A Sourcebook of New Methods*. Beverly Hills, Calif.: Sage.

Miller, D. 1991. *Handbook of Research Design and Social Measurement*. Newbury Park, Calif.: Sage.

Moore, R., Studenmundt, A., and Slobko, T. 1991. The effect of the financial aid package on the choice of a selective college. *Economics of Education Review* 10:311–21.

Orfield, G., and Paul, F. 1993. *High Hopes, Long Odds: A Major Report on Hoosier Teens and the American Dream*. Indianapolis: Indiana Youth Institute.

Parrish, R. 1979. *Survey of Educational Goals: Ocean County High School Juniors and Seniors*. Toms River, N.J.: Ocean County College.

Pascarella, E., and Terenzini, P. 1991. *How College Affects Students*. San Francisco: Jossey-Bass.

Paulsen, M. 1990. *College Choice: Understanding Student Enrollment Behavior.* Washington, D.C.: ERIC Clearinghouse on Higher Education and George Washington University.

Radner, R., and Miller, L. 1970. Demand and supply in U.S. higher education: A progress report. *American Economic Review* 30:327–34.

Rogoff, B. 1990. *Apprenticeship in Thinking: Cognitive Development in Social Context*. New York: Oxford University Press.

Rumberer, R. 1982. The influence of family background on education, earnings, and wealth. *Social Forces* 61:773–75.

Russell, C. 1980. *Survey of Grade 12 Students' Postsecondary Plans and Aspirations*. Manitoba: Canadian Department of Education.

Schmit, J. 1991. An empirical look at the search stage of the student college choice process. Paper presented at the annual meeting of the Association for the Study of Higher Education, Boston.

Schmit, J., and Hossler, D. 1995. Where are they now?: A nine-year longitudinal study of student college choice. Paper presented at the annual meeting of the American Educational Research Association, San Francisco.

Schultz, T. 1961. Educational and economic growth. In N. Henry, ed., *Social Forces Influencing American Education*. Chicago: National Society for the Study of Education.

Sewell, W., Haller, A., and Portes, A. 1969. The educational and early occupational attainment process. *American Sociological Review* 34:82–92.

Sewell, W., and Hauser, R. 1975. *Education, Occupation, and Earnings: Achievement in Early Career.* New York: Academic.

Sewell, W., and Shah, V. 1978. Social class, parental encouragement, and educational aspirations. *American Journal of Sociology* 3:559–72.

Sharp, S., Johnson, J., Kurotsuchi, K., and Waltman, J. 1996. Insider information: Social influences on college attendance. Paper presented at the annual meeting of the American Educational Research Association, San Francisco.

Sheppard, L., Schmit, J., and Pugh, R. 1992. Factors influencing high school students' changes in plans for post secondary education: A longitudinal study. Paper presented at the annual meeting of the American Educational Research Association, San Francisco.

St. John, E. 1991. The impact of student financial aid: A review of recent research. *Journal of Student Financial Aid* 21:18–32.

Stage, F., and Hossler, D. 1989. Differences in family influences on college attendance plans for male and female ninth graders. *Research in Higher Education* 30:301–14.

Stewart, N., et al. 1987. Counselor impact on college choice. Paper presented at the annual meeting of the American Educational Research Association, Washington, D.C.

Stinchcombe, A. 1990. *Information and Organizations.* Berkeley: University of California Press.

Tillery, D. 1973. *Distribution and Differentiation of Youth: A Study of Transition from School to College.* Cambridge: Ballinger.

Trent, J., and Medsker, L. 1967. *Beyond High School: A Psychological Study of 10,000 High School Graduates.* San Francisco: Jossey-Bass.

Trueman, R. 1977. *Introduction to Quantitative Methods for Decision Making.* New York: Holt, Rinehart, and Winston.

Tuttle, R. 1981. *A Path Analytical Model of the College-Going Decision.* Boone, N.C.: Appalachian State University.

Vesper, N., Hossler, D., and Bouse, G. 1991. The changing importance of college attributes: A longitudinal study. Paper presented at the annual meeting of the American Educational Research Association, Chicago.

Walberg, H. 1990. OECD indicators of educational productivity. *Educational Researcher* 19:30–33.

Weiss, L. 1990. *Working Class without Work: High School Students in a De-Industrialized Economy.* London: Routledge.

Yang, S. 1981. Rural youth's decisions to attend college: Aspirations and realizations. Paper presented at the annual meeting of the Rural Sociological Association, Guelph, Ontario.

Young, M., and Reyes, P. 1987. Conceptualizing enrollment behavior. *Journal of Student Financial Aid* 17:41–49.

Zemsky, R., and Oedel, P. 1983. *The Structure of College Choice.* New York: College Board.

Zey, M. 1992. *Decision Making: Alternatives to Rational Choice Models.* Newbury Park, Calif.: Sage

Index

Library of Congress Cataloging-in-Publication Data

Hossler, Don.

Going to college : how social, economic, and educational factors influence the decisions students make / Don Hossler, Jack Schmit, and Nick Vesper.

p. cm.

Includes bibliographical references (p.) and index.

ISBN 0-8018-6000-8 (alk. paper).—ISBN 0-8018-6001-6 (pbk. : alk. paper)

1. College choice—Social aspects—Indiana—Longitudinal studies. 2. High school students—Indiana—Social conditions—Longitudinal studies. 3. Student aspirations—Indiana—Longitudinal studies. I. Schmit, Jack L. II. Vesper, Nick. III. Title.

LB2350.5.H634 1998

378.1′61—dc21 98-25006

CIP